Wyoming Mountains & Home-waters

Wyoming Mountains & Home-waters

FAMILY, FLY FISHING, AND CONSERVATION

Bradley Johnson

Sage Creek Press
Cody, WY

Wyoming Mountains & Home-waters
Family, Fly Fishing, and Conservation
Bradley Johnson
Sage Creek Press
2549 Newton Ave.
Cody, WY 82414
Copyright © 2017 by Sage Creek Press, LLC
www.sagecreekpress.com

First Edition
ISBN: 0998893404
ISBN: 9780998893402
eBook: ISBN: 978-0-9988934-1-9
Library of Congress Control Number: 2017906335
Sage Creek Press, LLC
Cover photo by Bradley Johnson
Cover and interior design by Createspace

I have tried to recreate events, locales, and conversations from my memories of them. In some instances, I have changed or omitted the names of individuals and places in order to maintain their anonymity, and I may have changed some identifying characteristics and details, such as physical properties, occupations, and places of residence.

For Bailee and Gabriel

Contents

Acknowledgments

DURING THE SIX YEARS THAT it took for this project to come to fruition, more people assisted me with inspiration, support, and data than I could possibly hope to thank here—so if you don't see your name, please know that your efforts have not gone unappreciated.

I would like to begin by thanking Roy and Nancy Johnson for introducing Brandon and me to the family cabin, setting in place my love of fly fishing and the outdoors. I would also like to offer a brotherly thanks to Brandon for taking so much of this journey in life with me.

Thank you to Tom and Cheryl Shultz and Johanna Cubbage for the many cups of coffee and the many family stories about Rubyat. Thank you to Mitch Kalter and Mark Seymour from Great Bay Trout Unlimited, for taking a Wyoming kid under their wing and introducing me to New England waters, trout, and conservation ethics. Thank you to the many dedicated scientists and resource managers with the Wyoming Game and Fish Department, with a special thanks to Tim Woolley, Sam Hochhalter, and Jason Burckhardt. Thank you to the Hot Springs County Museum and Cultural Center for helping me discover obscure resources.

Thank you, Mimi Becker, for your endless patience and mentorship—this book is a direct outcome of your faith in me. Thank you, Tom Lee, for introducing me to the science of ecology and fostering that love during my tenure as a graduate student at the University of New Hampshire. A big thank you to my labmate Dave Howland for providing reviews, comments, and insights on early materials for the project. I must give a big thanks to my mom for passing along her love of reading, which has translated, for me, into a love of writing. The penultimate thank you goes to my editors, Cheryl Nicchitta and Christina Palaia, for whose attention to detail I'm exceedingly grateful.

Finally, I want to thank my wife, Trista, for her boundless support throughout this endeavor—without your encouragement, this project would never have been realized.

Thank you, all!

Prologue: Iraq, 2004

THE INDUSTRY OF WAR IS shrouded in endless cacophony, even when operating at its slowest tempo. Beyond the intermittent burst of gunfire and explosions that accompany heavy weaponry there lies the constant and ceaseless humming of the ubiquitous diesel engine. It was this noise that enveloped me as I walked from our sand-colored tent—one in a row of tents, which was itself one of many, many rows of identically lined-up tents—to the motor pool where our platoon's vehicles sat between missions. Tanks, massive trucks, the iconic Humvee, and our modified personnel carrier all roared with diesel engines. It mattered little whether it was night or day: these engines roared throughout. At night, they would be joined by enormous generators humming along and powering the massive camp, from the air conditioning that provided relief to soldiers who had been out on patrol all day, trapped in ceramic-plated body armor in the Middle Eastern sun and heat, to the computer systems that gave our army its information and technological advantage over our adversaries.

The aluminum-bodied Cold War monstrosity that was our vehicle had been cleaned, repaired, and outfitted for the next mission, while the detritus of the last patrol—the MRE wrappers, Gatorade bottles, and guts of torn sandbags meant to blunt the impact of deadly shrapnel from IEDs—had been removed. We were about to prepare for our next mission by loading up food and water, ammunition, and first-aid kits and by going through our precombat checks and inspections to ensure our own personal and team readiness for the mission.

Our missions were euphemistically termed "route-clearing." What this term meant in reality was that our platoon would fan out on both sides of the road in an attempt to discover where IEDs may have been laid the night before. We would walk slowly, watching for where earth had been disturbed or where something, particularly trash, looked out of place, which could indicate that an IED might have been hidden there. We were each keenly aware that IEDs capable of shredding vehicles would easily do the same to our bodies, and this knowledge would cause us to keep extra distance between each member of the platoon as we grimly walked along Iraq's trash-strewn roads.

My route to this moment had been circuitous. I had been assigned to the 1st Armored Division when I arrived in Germany for my first overseas tour with the army. Initially the thought was that my role in Iraq would be to assist with the division's transition back to Germany. By the time I arrived in Iraq in January 2004, the unit I was joining, a field artillery outfit, had already been in Iraq for almost a year, and many assumed that major combat operations were over and that we were transitioning to what were called "stability operations"—an amorphous term that reflected the lack of definable goals and objectives that followed the highly successful march to Baghdad in 2003.

But all that changed with the insurgency that followed the destruction of the Iraqi army and the collapse of the government. The insurgency, which exploded throughout Baghdad and many other portions of Iraq in the spring of 2004, put military planners on their heels, as they scrambled to adequately respond to an unanticipated new enemy. The 1st Armored Division's tour in Iraq was extended, initially indefinitely, rather than wrapping up after a year's worth of combat. Following the extension of that tour, the 4th Battalion of the 27th Field Artillery Regiment, of which I was a member, left Forward Operating Base Thunder in Baghdad for BIAP (the army loves acronyms, and this particular one was short for Baghdad International Airport). It was the increasingly deadly insurgency and its reliance on cheap and effective IEDs that, in part, resulted in the 4/27th Field Artillery still operating in Iraq in the spring of 2004 rather than redeploying back to Germany.

That morning, as I made the familiar journey from tent to motor pool, I noticed that spring in Iraq was bringing with it temperatures I was more used to experiencing during the summer in my home state of Wyoming, and with the early heat came black flies and mosquitoes. Just before entering our vehicle, as one of the final preparations for our next mission, I sprayed a small amount of insect repellent into my hand to rub on my face. The scent brought with it an unexpected blow of homesickness. It was a scent that had the power to transport me back to Wyoming—not to the tiny two-bedroom trailer-house that had, for far too long, housed my brother Brandon and me, our five step-siblings, and our mom and second stepfather but, instead, to the small three-room log cabin in the mountains of Wyoming that had been a respite from the chaos of our dilapidated and overcrowded trailer-house. In that moment, I was transported across oceans and through time, back to my childhood—back to a little log cabin called Rubyat in the Bighorn Mountains of Wyoming and to the land and waters surrounding the cabin: a pine-tree-covered hillside, a mountain meadow, and a quarter mile of crystalline trout stream.

During my childhood, my escape from the crush of poverty had been found in weekends spent with my grandparents and, if it was summertime and I was lucky, trips to the family cabin built by the hand of my great-great-grandfather, Ruby Shultz, in the summers of 1916 and 1917. Affectionately known on my father's side of the family as Rubyat, the cabin was my childhood salvation from life in a tiny trailer-house with eight other members of my family, but it would be the quarter mile of trout stream that flowed below the cabin that would capture my soul and, unbeknownst to me at the time, guide my life and my career. It would be at Rubyat that I would make my lifelong connection to nature; the snowmelt mountain stream flowing below the hill from the cabin would become my home-waters, and upon those home-waters my connection to nature would be cemented through the sport of fly fishing.

The hold on me that these quiet waters have, which came to me so clearly that day in Iraq, even through the cacophony of the war, has only grown during the subsequent decades. In the chapters that follow, I attempt to trace the ways in which these waters have shaped and continue to shape my life and the life of my family.

Part I

CHAPTER 1

Home-waters & Fly Fishing

THE STORY OF MY LIFE cannot be separated from my love of trout and fly fishing and conservation. The first time my grandfather roused me to take me fly fishing on the stream below the cabin, I was eight years old and happily unaware that fly fishing was supposed to be a sport of the wealthy and elite. In fact, unless I was spending a weekend with my grandparents, it was rare in those days for my family to be able to afford a haircut, let alone unsoiled clothes free of holes. In the years after my introduction to fly fishing, my trips to the cabin would be marked by an almost uncontainable childhood excitement for getting on the water; this was followed by the focus and determination required to find the right fly pattern, read the water, make the cast, and then, when luck and skill tentatively overlapped, finally be rewarded by a strike from a rising trout. The beauty and tenacity of the trout that inhabited the waters below the cabin would be central to my enjoyment of fly fishing. And the pursuit of brook, brown, and rainbow trout during Wyoming summers on the stream, surrounded by towering lodgepole pine trees filled with chattering red squirrels, would occupy my daydreams throughout the school year.

The stream below the cabin was always filled with trout ready to, at the least, look at my fly, if not strike at it, following a clumsy childhood cast. As a child, I never thought to question why there were so many trout ready to take my proffered meal of feathers, thread, and sharpened hook. I always marveled at how the species of trout would change not only between days of fishing on the same water but between catches. I never knew, until I brought it to hand, if the trout that had been fooled on a particular cast was a small but gaudily colored brook trout, a vibrant and feisty rainbow trout, or a stubborn and muted-palette brown trout.

It wouldn't be until many years later, while I was in graduate school, that I would understand that the plentitude of fish I had encountered as a child was likely the result of artificial propagation through fish hatcheries that churned out trout on an industrial scale. It would come as a shock to me to realize that not a single species of trout I had once eagerly waited to lay eyes on, as I fought them at the end of my line, was native to my home-waters.

After coming home from overseas with the army, I pursued a master's degree in political science, which involved studying the policy and management related to Yellowstone cutthroat trout. It was then that I became aware of the difference between hatchery-stocked, wild, and native trout. This taste of ecology was enough to convince me to pursue a doctorate, which allowed me to study ecology, climate change, and public land management in greater detail. Both graduate degrees would give me the opportunity to conduct research in the Rocky Mountains, which, in turn, would reconnect me to the mountain waters of my youth.

My research also made me aware, for the first time, of the global issue of habitat loss and species extinction, which would again bring me back to the trout that inhabited my home-waters. Native trout are in danger of extinction throughout the world but are particularly endangered in the western United States, including in the two ecosystems I knew best growing up: the Bighorn Mountains and the Greater Yellowstone Ecosystem of Wyoming.

The trout native to my home-waters is the Yellowstone cutthroat trout, not the brook, brown, or rainbow trout I knew so well as a child. As I began to appreciate the differences between native and non-native species, I also developed an appreciation for the differences between native and wild trout, and how both were an altogether difference class of fish from the hatchery-raised trout stocked into streams, rivers, lakes, and ponds, oft-times to be pulled from the water in a single season. The reason I had never caught a native trout when I was growing up is that they have been enveloped in the global trend of species decline and extinction. The trout native to my home-waters below Rubyat are locally extinct and can no longer be found within that watershed. While the brook, brown, and rainbow trout that I caught as a child and that I continue to cast to today are not natives of my home-waters, I do not begrudge them their non-native distinction. Rather, I wish to demonstrate my appreciation by instead recognizing the trout that are native to my home-waters and then providing an ecosystem-spanning strategy for their conservation and eventual return.

A DOSE OF CONSERVATION HERESY

It is true that there is no shortage of trout you can cast a fly, lure, or dunk a worm for in waters throughout the United States. But native trout—now that is a different story entirely. While I never lament any trout that finds itself fooled by my hook wrapped in feathers, thread, and tinsel, I have become much more sensitive to which trout are native to the waters I'm fishing and which have home ranges in another part of the country or, in the case of brown trout, another continent. Likewise, my love of fly fishing has not been lessened because I catch non-native trout, but the thrill of the catch has been exponentially heightened when I catch trout that have evolved in those same waters and landscapes that I'm fishing.

Without overlooking the tremendous amount of progress that has been made to restore damaged and fragmented trout habitat throughout the country, we need to recognize that we have entered an unparalleled era when human impacts are global but often manifest visibly within the ecosystems we frequent when pursuing outdoor recreational activities. Habitat fragmentation and outright habitat loss; pollution; and the introduction, establishment, and spread of invasive species: all act synergistically to undermine the fragile ecosystems trout reside within. Our ecosystems are imperiled by the razing of physical and ecological processes, including the permanent unhinging of the water cycle and the disruption of disturbance regimes, such as the role of wildfire and floods. This destruction undermines the resilience of ecosystems while simultaneously revealing the vital connections between aquatic environments and healthy upland ecosystems, whether that be mountain forests, grasslands, or sagebrush steppe. Exacerbating all these problems is global climate change, which affects each of these environs at the national, ecosystem, and local levels.

Today we are ecologically and culturally poorer for the extinction of two entire species of trout native to the western United States. In a world of global environmental impacts, if we are to be successful in preventing more of our native trout species from sliding into extinction, we must ensure that the ecosystems in which native trout and their habitat reside are not only healthy but resilient. This requires that we expand our view of coldwater conservation to include the uplands that surround our favorite trout waters, which ensure their health or contribute to their decline. It also requires that we commit to conserving the top-tier predators—yes, carnivores—that are essential to maintaining healthy ecosystems. It is my hope that I can demonstrate that preserving an ecological system requires maintaining all of its elements, even those that have previously been seen as superfluous or as a threat.

My proposal to elevate native trout over wild non-natives may be seen as nothing less than conservation heresy by some. It is not my intention to cast aspersions upon the tremendous work that has successfully restored wild trout habitat and allowed wild populations of beautiful trout to flourish. But today we are within the throes of the sixth great extinction, and we must recognize that the native trout that make our waters unique are beginning to be caught within the vortex of global biodiversity loss. If we are to seriously address this worldwide crisis for our favorite coldwater species, we must recognize the role non-native wild trout populations play in undermining the ecological security of native trout.

Volumes of elegant words have been spun together to pay homage to trout, nature, and fly fishing. My words are more humble in their origin and composition, and the best that I can hope for is that my tale of childhood love of cabin, trout, and fly fishing is worthy of demonstrating the need for protection, conservation, and restoration of native trout. My individual story begins on one small home-water in Wyoming, but my experience there is a single gossamer silk thread in a global tapestry of biodiversity—an ecological masterpiece that we are trying to preserve even as humanity continues to pull at loose strands while ignobly cutting others altogether. Fly fishing for trout on a Wyoming stream saved a little boy from rural poverty; I hope to repay that debt herein.

CHAPTER 2

Wyoming Poverty

Wyoming has always prided itself on its rugged individualism and low population density; a longstanding point of pride was the claim that there were more cattle in Wyoming than people. The state has worked hard to burnish its image as a place where the cowboy way of life from the turn of the nineteenth century was still intact—of a rugged and unpopulated landscape, with an economy built upon ranching and farming. Of course, this image is mostly myth, and it is the energy development industry that has long driven the state economy.

In the Bighorn Basin that has been home to four generations of my family, many of the oilfields are over one hundred years old. Oil, gas, and coal are what bring wealth to the state and what the legislature depends upon to balance its budget. In the Basin, the oil-patch has always held sought-after jobs, and in decades past, these jobs—including some high-paying ones—could be attained without so much as a high school diploma. But like all things that appear too good to be true, Wyoming's energy sector also has a dark side: when the pendulum swings from boom to bust, there is little to turn to, other than government assistance and the sympathy of fellow community members who have long known that with every good time comes an eventual crash.

The Bighorn Basin is a microcosm of Wyoming and is home to both agriculture and significant oil and gas resources. No town in the Bighorn Basin has been spared the effects of the energy industry's boom-bust cycle, and it has become apparent with each swing of the pendulum that the busts are running longer and leaving deeper collective social scars. Although I've never seen it, there is supposedly a bumper sticker that reads "God, please let there be one more boom—this time I promise not to piss it away!" This tongue-in-cheek prayer captures the community's cultural bipolarity about being so deeply dependent on the energy sector for the entirety of its well-being. Wealth and security are created by each boom; struggle and despair accompany each bust.

I have often wondered how much of my childhood followed the vagaries of the energy sector. I do know that stability and security were never qualities my brother or I experienced during our childhood. After our parents divorced, we found ourselves skipping across the Bighorn Basin from one town to the next, in the tow of our mother's relationships. Lovell, Greybull, Thermopolis, Cody, and then the hamlet of Byron: each town was briefly home, but only as long as it held a job or a relationship. I learned as a child that in the Basin, neither jobs nor relationships were all that enduring.

In Lovell, before I entered kindergarten, we lived on a street that wasn't paved. In Greybull, I remember making my first playground friend in elementary school. When we moved to Greybull with our first stepfather, we lived in a trailer-house eerily similar to the one we would live in a few years later with our second stepfamily. It was located on a street directly across from the railroad tracks that ran through town and was tucked along the outside edge of a meander of the Bighorn River.

It was also in Greybull that I first remember going on government assistance. It was an unusual evening in that we were walking together as a family. The humidity and the mosquitoes hung heavy in the long rays of the summer evening. Our walk took us to the door of a local church, which we had never visited before. Laid out on tables throughout were despairingly plain white-packaged foodstuffs of all sorts. Bold black writing identified what was contained within each package, which were unencumbered by advertising or color—crackers, cheese, rice, and powdered milk. Beans and coffee came in silver cans without labels, and with the same depressing black writing. I remember my parents hesitantly picking items from the tables and placing them in paper bags. The walk back home was quiet and sullen. We would return intermittently throughout the year, and the plain-packaged food would fill the cupboards even more during the winter months.

In Thermopolis I entered the second grade and made a new set of school friends; I also learned that hot springs came with the smell of sulfur and that if you were fast enough you might be able to grab one of the pennies that people threw into the rainbow-hued hot spring pools for luck. Thermopolis introduced me to the challenges of being part of a new family for the first time, and it was where I also learned the harsher lessons of alcohol, anger, and—for the second time—the hurt of divorce.

At the end of my third-grade year, we moved to Cody, where I regained some family: a grandpa, aunts, uncles, and cousins, as well as a new school that this time felt very alien. There was an odd feeling that came with living in our fourth new town, an artificiality to it, a child's understanding that it wouldn't last. The rollercoaster of towns would finally end soon after we were introduced to our second stepfather. After he and my mom were married, we left Cody for Byron: our fifth town in little more than six years.

Population 470—that was the number of people living in Byron, according to the white-and-green sign that stood at the edge of town. Even in Wyoming, which had a total population of just over 450,000 in 1990, the year we moved to Byron, the town was considered a rural burg. I was ten and would attend the fifth grade at the start of the school year. The "main street" was U.S. Highway 14A, which ran through the middle of town. There were no stoplights, although as you entered the town limits, the speed limit changed from sixty-five miles an hour to thirty. I suspect that the only reason for even this attenuation was because both the town's school and its largest church, the two most dominant buildings in the hamlet, sat directly on the highway.

With our new stepfather, we had also gained a new family—again. The core of our family had always been Brandon, Mom, and me, even when our mother had remarried the first time. Although our first stepfather had two children of his own, we only saw them during the summer, and we had sort of enjoyed having other children around, especially since the relationship was short-term and unburdened by the constant competition for attention that can come with the melding of new families. Brandon and I quickly learned that the same wasn't going to be true of our new stepfamily.

The man who would become our second stepfather had five children of his own from two previous marriages. The early combination of the two families was a riotous and ever-shifting combination of kids from his first two marriages. The oldest was my age (about nine) and the youngest was a toddler still in diapers. No longer was having a stepfamily going to be a short-term summertime adventure. In this new household, up to seven children (the number shifted depending on whether our new stepfather had custodial responsibility for one or more of his children on any given day) often competed for my mother's attention in our tiny trailer-house. Add to this an intense sibling rivalry and bottle it up in a household too small for so many people and you have the making of misery.

Neither our mom nor our new stepfather had a high school diploma. In Wyoming this did not necessarily sentence you to poverty if you could land one of the well-paying jobs in the oil-patch, but there were limits to what those jobs could accomplish for a family of nine. For us, it meant living in a two-bedroom sheet-aluminum trailer-house. The six boys in the family were roomed together in the back bedroom of the trailer. Because there was only enough space for two sets of bunk beds and a saggy foldaway bed, a rotation schedule determined who would sleep on which bed and who would sleep on the floor each night. Our parents had the bedroom nearest the front door of the dwelling. My only stepsister slept on the living-room couch outside of their room.

"Good pay for hard work" has always been an unspoken motto in rural Wyoming. Going hand-in-hand with that silent expectation was also an understanding that it wasn't necessary to have a college degree or even a high school diploma for hard work to be rewarded. After we moved to Byron and even though we lived in a trailer-house again, things initially seemed like they were looking up. Our new stepfather found employment as a field hand in the nearby oilfield, and his grandparents lived close by. The Byron oilfield, like most oilfields in the Bighorn Basin, is an old field, having first been tapped around 1918 for the hydrocarbons held beneath the soil. But the rapidly globalizing markets of the early 1990s cared little for age or cultural heritage, as the oil sector slipped into a bust market and prices plummeted.

Lower prices meant less drilling, which meant less need for workers in the oil-patch. The first to go were the field hands. My stepfather quickly found another job, although a less lucrative one, working on a local hog farm, but that work came to an abrupt end one winter's day when he sustained a back injury, which would end up becoming a lifelong disability. If it had not been for a loose hog and an errant step on ice, our family situation may not have been untenable, although feeding seven growing children just by the sweat of one's brow is a tall order. Perhaps this would not have been a terminal sentence of poverty if there had been fewer children or if either my mom or stepfather had held a high school diploma—but these were significant barriers, and they would keep us tethered in poverty after that fateful winter day.

While that sultry summer evening in Greybull walking to the unfamiliar church was my first experience with government assistance, it wasn't my last. Food stamps, Social Security, and free school lunches would become a regular part of my life following my second stepfather's worksite accident. Often we would crowd around our little dinner table, with each served an equal portion that wasn't enough to satisfy the hunger of a growing child; all too often, we would leave the table with food in our stomachs, but not full. Breakfasts were often just as bleak—although, looking back, I realize it is a testament to the organizational capabilities and will of our parents that they were able to get all seven of us children fed, even if with just a piece of toast or a small bowl of cold cereal, before getting us off to school. Our poverty made us thankful for the free school lunches that ensured we would have three meals a day. While no child loves all that is plopped upon their tray by the school lunch lady, I had left the dinner table hungry far too many times to take for granted a full lunch made available to me in the school cafeteria.

SMALL-TOWN SELF-RELIANCE

Although both poverty and, eventually, government assistance became an inevitable part of our lives, so was the virtue of self-reliance, which was imbued in all of us by both our parents and our community. It's part of the Wyoming spirit. In meeting the often Sisyphean challenge of ensuring that all seven of us had enough to eat, our family relied on wild game as an important part of our diet, year-round. Hunting and fishing are engrained in the culture of my family, as well as in the culture of Wyoming, and deer, elk, and fish were staples of our diet whenever they were available. Each of us took to hunting and fishing in our own way. My desire to hunt has waxed and waned over the years, but fishing—even before I learned to fly fish—has always been one of my favorite activities.

When I was growing up, we would often take family excursions to go rabbit hunting. When we reached double digits in age, we were allowed to accompany our stepfather when he went deer hunting. With six boys in the family, it wasn't a requirement that each of us go hunting, though, and I opted out, choosing instead to stick with fishing. It wouldn't be until years later that I would take up hunting as an excuse to come home to Wyoming and reconnect with friends and family.

One summer, after returning to live in Wyoming, I attended a summer barbeque with some of my extended family and found myself sitting in the shade of our host's porch discussing my work in natural resource management. A cousin shared with the assembled family: "It used to be back in the day that if a man was down on his luck, the community would turn a blind eye to him poaching a deer or two to feed his family, but you don't dare do that today. No sir, the penalties are too stiff." There was murmured agreement on this point. As I reflect on that conversation, I can't help but wonder how often, during the leanest of times, we were fed with an unlucky deer that had been poached in the dark of night on a lonely back road—and whether this was one of the many ways that the community, recognizing the pervasiveness of poverty, not only in my family but throughout the community, quietly helped us.

Fishing pole, hook, line, bobber, worm: these are the tools I first learned to fish with and the ones that were familiar to my immediate family. I never had anything against chucking a worm into the deep waters of the local reservoirs and waiting for a perch, bluegill, trout, or catfish to bite. More often than not, it would be some form of sucker or carp that would take my bait. These "trash" fish, if they were lucky, were thrown back in the water; if unlucky, they were used as cut-bait on a hook to replace the worm they had eaten. The nearby Yellowtail Reservoir was a favorite destination of my family. What I remember most about trips to the reservoir wasn't the fishing but the burning summer sun under a cloudless sky with not a lick of wind to temper the heat. It was custom during those trips to try to catch and keep your maximum limit of fish so that they could be tossed in the freezer and saved for as many meals as could be squeezed from their piscine bodies.

The summer that I graduated from bait fishing to fly fishing was a seminal event for me. Independence of thoughts, ideas, and actions were highly valued by my family, and my transition to fly fishing was quickly accepted by my parents. I have often wondered if my family's acceptance of independent ideas and actions was a function of the size of my family or if it was a hallmark of raising a family in small-town Wyoming. Whatever the case, my stepfather took an interest in my new passion and was supportive of it, even when it meant my fishing experience differed from the rest of the family's. This forbearance became particularly significant when I began practicing catch-and-release, since I was allowing food to slip through my fingers and back into the waters. My parents didn't once question my decision to release the fish I caught; in fact, they supported it without hesitation, even when it meant not filling my creel limit. Although fly fishing set me apart when on the stream with my immediate family, it also empowered me and sharpened my connection to nature. I recognize today that this experience would never have been possible without my family's support, even and especially during difficult times when my fly fishing practices could have resulted in potential hunger for the family later in the year.

WYOMING WINTER, WARM BLANKETS

Although the oilfield lying just outside of town would no longer offer us relief for our poverty, it reached into our lives nonetheless. During summer evenings when we kept every window wide open to help alleviate the heat that the aluminum siding had captured and poured into the trailer all day long, the smell of sulfur would waft into town and through the open windows of our small trailer-house. During the winter, on certain evenings when the wind was at its most still and every sound seemed like it could carry for miles, you could hear the steady *tump-tump-tump* of the iron-headed pump jacks working ceaselessly in the nearby oilfield. The coldest and calmest winter nights offered the perfect conditions to transmit the sound from the oilfield across town and in through the closed, plastic-covered window in our crowded back bedroom.

A wood-burning stove in the living room at the other end of the trailer was stoked to the fullest all day long to heat the thin-skinned house. At night, after the fire in the stove burned down to ash and smoldering embers, a natural gas-fired heater was allowed to heat the house—but only enough to keep the heat-taped water lines from freezing and bursting, and ample blankets were required to keep warm throughout the night. When morning came and the light to the bedroom was flipped on to tell us it was time to get dressed for school, we only grudgingly left our warm beds to enter the early morning cold, getting into clothes and coats as fast as possible.

One bitter cold and windless night, I lay on the saggy foldaway bed beneath the window, listening to the rhythmic *tump-tump-tump* of the distant pump jacks as I tried to fall asleep. The house had cooled off considerably since I had gone to bed. A noise in the room caught my attention—someone had gotten up. I poked my head out of the blankets to see who it was. I didn't see anyone moving through the room; what I saw instead was Brandon's blanket heaped on the floor.

Our grandmother who took us to the cabin had woven blankets for both Brandon and me. Mine was green and white, his brown and gold. His little blanket was on the floor, with him underneath it, even though it wasn't his turn to sleep there. As I tried to make sense of what I was seeing, I realized he was lying on top of the only heater vent in the cramped bedroom, waiting for the heater to kick on again and provide a little relief from the cold. I remember wishing he would just crawl back into bed; he would have found the warmth there far sooner than waiting for the intermittent heat that came from the little vent cut in the floor. As I watched my little brother huddled forlornly over a tiny heater vent in the floor, I couldn't help but wonder how our lives had come to this. The depressing sight of that cold Wyoming night has stayed with me for over twenty years.

CHAPTER 3

Rubyat

THE CHALLENGE OF MELDING TOGETHER two families is trying in the best of situations. My mother's willingness to go from mom to two children to mom and stepmother to seven is a testament to her enduring patience and boundless capacity for love. Another of her great acts of love was her encouragement of a wonderful relationship between Brandon and me and our dad's parents. It is no small feat for someone to look past the hurt and bitterness following the emotional schism of divorce and put their children first. The relationship we had with them is also a testament to one of the qualities that make grandparents, grandparents—unconditional love of grandchildren, regardless of the parents' marital status. I have seen the same pattern play out time and time again, as grandparents become the stabilizing force in a child's life after the trauma of a divorce.

Our mom made sure that Brandon and I were able to visit and spend time with our grandparents, no matter the distances involved and even as we moved from town to town through the Bighorn Basin. After remarrying for the second time, she recognized that time spent with Grandma and Grandpa was often the escape we needed in order to find balance in our lives as we sought to navigate the turbulence of our second stepfamily in only a few years. Their house in Worland, Wyoming, was a love-filled respite from the cramped and contentious trailer-house. Whether a quick weekend trip or an entire summer, visits to Grandma and Grandpa's house were a salve for the soul, as there is nothing more nurturing than the gentle love of a grandparent.

Summertime trips became the highlight of the year for me, as this meant we could travel up the looming Bighorn Mountains to Rubyat. Although our first trips to Rubyat were surprise adventures, as we got older, I began to make insistent, vocal requests; fortunately, it took very little beseeching to convince my grandparents to pack the car and take the hour-long trip to the cabin.

EXPLORING NATURE

My home-waters, if traced to their utmost beginnings, originate in the snows that occupy the heights of the Bighorn Mountains. These mountains, which dominate the eastern horizon of the Bighorn Basin, are a sister range to the more famous Absaroka-Beartooths that serve as the western boundary of the Basin and are home to Yellowstone National Park. The oil-rich Bighorn Basin stretches between the two, occupying nearly 10,000 square miles, and runs 120 miles north to south and 60 miles east to west, generally speaking, of course.[1] Both the Absaroka-Beartooths and the Bighorn Mountains owe their existence to the mountain-building epoch of the Laramide orogeny that began in the late Cretaceous period and continued through the early Eocene, 35–80 million years ago. Though separated by the Bighorn Basin, both are part of the Rocky Mountains. While the two are sister ranges, each has its own distinct personality, which is reflected in the waters that flow from their slopes. From the Bighorn Mountains flow many tributaries to the world-renowned Bighorn River, including Tensleep Creek, which flows past the cabin; the Absaroka-Beartooths are home to a number of famous rivers, including the Yellowstone, Madison, and Firehole, to name just a few.

Every time we drove up the Bighorn Mountains, leaving behind the sweltering Basin heat, I could hardly wait to catch my first glimpse of crystal-clear snowmelt waters. As we traversed the route to the cabin, I would stare out the car window looking for any hint of the beautiful stream. Driving east we would pass through the quaint town of Ten Sleep before entering the canyon bearing the same name, which was my indicator that we were on the cusp of entering the mountains. Tensleep Canyon is a narrow cut in the base of the mountains filled with streamside willows, massive cottonwood trees, and the non-native Russian olive trees that were loved by pioneers for their hardiness and are fed by the waters of Tensleep and Leigh Creeks.

Just before the steep switchbacks that climb up the side of the mountain to deposit you on the top, there is a sign for the Ten Sleep Fish Hatchery. It is the location of one of my only memories of my mom and dad together while they were still married. As the four of us walked among the ponds on the tree-covered hatchery grounds, with Leigh Creek flowing past us just a short distance away, my parents had given me a slice of white bread to form into balls in my child-sized fists, so that I could feed the massive hatchery trout swimming in the pools. As is often the case, the circumstances just prior to the unfortunate incident have been lost to memory; what I do remember is that one moment I was standing on the grassy bank of the pond throwing bread to the trout and the next I was in their pool splashing and screaming. Most likely, my parents' attention was focused on Brandon, who was just transitioning to toddlerhood. As my dad was still scrambling to reach me, I was plucked out of the pond by a friendly tourist, who must have seen the entire incident. I remember that I was still tightly holding a soggy ball of bread in my hand, but some of the bread had come apart while I was thrashing in the water, and I watched as the enormous fish in the pond, only momentarily spooked, began to plod their way toward the bread I had left behind.

Ascending the switchbacks meant that we had left the Basin behind and were officially in the mountains. More importantly, it meant we were now in the mountain forests that held the cabin. There I could explore the natural world on my own terms; I was alone but also at my fullest. There was no competition or fighting with my stepsiblings to keep my mind tethered to the here and now. There was no embarrassment about going to school in clothes that had been donated to a charity in the 1970s. Under the boughs of the evergreens, I shed my skin of fear, anxiety, anger, and embarrassment for that of a world-class explorer. I could venture into the pine trees to discover tremendous multihued fungi growing out of the aromatic soil. Beneath the verdant eye of the forest surrounding the cabin, I was rewarded every time I discovered a new animal trail. I could let my imagination run wild while alone in the woods. A massive boulder became a fortress and a stick became a sword in a play game of soldier. The darker shadows cast by the closed canopy of evergreens hid archers, as I was transformed into a knight.

My imagination did not extend to thoughts about ecology or the health of a forest. The animal trails that I followed entered and exited evergreen stands, wet meadows, barrens, and riparian stream edges, but terms like these meant nothing to me back then. The flowers in bloom, thick-stemmed willows with the bark stripped, the stump of a beaver-chewed tree: these were the things that captured my eye and attention, teaching me about the natural world even as I played in an imaginary one. I spent hours watching the dam on the stream below the cabin, hoping to catch a glimpse of one of the beavers denning in the wood-and-mud lodge nearby, while songbirds called from hidden perches above.

The stream held all manner of discoveries during my explorer outings. The nature of the stream itself—cold, clear, constantly flowing without interruption—drew me to it in a way nothing else did. The sound of the rush of water over river cobble called to me, and the sight of the clear waters surrounded by the green of grass, willows, and trees set my young soul at peace. I would compare rocks taken from the edge of the stream and then delight in the unexpected discovery of aquatic insects clinging to their underside. Many of the insects looked like something from a late-night horror movie. I quickly learned that the rough yet slimy-bodied things could tenaciously grip the surface of the stone I held in my little hand. Decades later I would learn the remarkable role those dream-stirring little beasties played in the stream I had drawn them from, as they proved to be a steady source of food for the trout I would pursue with rod and reel.

A WAITING FRIEND

Each return to the cabin brought with it a panoply of anticipated and desired experiences. They would begin when the cabin came into view from the rutted two-track road, first as a dark brown visage hidden within the long shadows of towering lodgepole pines. As the pines thinned, they would reveal the wonderful old fellow, sitting majestically on the hillside, overlooking the meadow and with the stream hidden among the trees down below. Once the car was parked next to the cabin, I would dive out, to be greeted by the smell of the forest, which, depending on the time of year, was often awash with the pungent scent of lodgepole pine pollen. The vibrant sounds of birds both near and far brought together the sights, smells, and sounds of the living forest; they were joined by the rapid tap of the woodpecker overhead and the familiar chatter of the red squirrels as they scolded us from atop nearby trees. But the sound I was most interested in was too distant to be heard from the back door of the cabin. After receiving permission from my grandparents, who knew I was ready to burst with excitement to say hello to an old friend, I would storm down the well-trod path to the edge of the mountain stream that flowed past the path's terminus.

With a keen eye for change, I would nod to the new willow growth along the edges of the stream's banks. I would note where the high and rapid waters of the spring runoff had pushed debris up on the shore and created new undercut banks. Just beyond the end of the path, five or six feet into the stream, depending on how deep the water was running that day, an island lay my side of center channel. I would scan the long narrow island for changes while looking for a path out to it that would keep my worn-out tennis shoes and faded jeans from getting wet so early in the trip. Stepping from rock to rock where the bulk of each irregular cobble was still underwater, I would carefully make my way across the small side channel to the grass-laden island. The nature of the island changed every year, as rushing meltwaters from the spring thaw would deposit enormous tree trunks upon it one year, only to sweep them away the next. Some years, thick mats of tall grass would grow across the entirety of the narrow island, while other years, the grass would be confined to the narrow, high ridge that ran along the edge of the island closest to the shore.

My immediate interest beyond the island was the stream itself. I would take note of new logs deposited in the stream channel during the past year's runoff, which had also swept away older logs, changing the complexity of the water. Less dramatic, but no less important to a young fly fisherman, were shifts in the willows, whose supple branches overhung the stream in many places. Most important, though, was the depth of the water in the stream itself. Water depth, velocity, and temperature would determine just how much time I could spend on the stream fly fishing and where I could go and with how much supervision. I would take all this in and quickly say hello to this gently chuckling friend before skipping back across the rocks to the nearby shore. Then, as I made my way back up the short trail to the cabin, I would begin to plan the weekend's fishing.

After unpacking food for the weekend (including such goodies as marshmallows to roast while sitting in front of the fireplace and York peppermint patties to enjoy while fishing) and placing the suitcases of dry clothes on the appropriate bed (to be reserved for changing into after wading in the stream), I'd take out the fishing gear, which we stored outside on the workbench. Here each rod would be assembled, lines stretched from reels, and leaders attached. During this enterprise Grandpa would join me, providing words of wisdom about what fly to tie on and how to be safe while on the water. His words were always spoken with a gentle sternness that combined wisdom and grandfatherly love. Fishing by myself was great, but fishing with Grandpa was an opportunity never to be passed up.

First Fish

The first time that Grandpa took me fly fishing, the air was sharp, with the chill of the previous night hanging heavy in the thick shadows of the early morning. My warm breath floated as vapor before me as I stood at my grandfather's side, watching intently and shivering in the morning chill as he ran a clear, thin monofilament leader through the eye of the fly he held in his hand. It was a small black fly with a pearl white feather, which served as wings, and a tail of red; he informed me that it was called a black gnat and that it was one of my grandmother's favorite flies. "It tends to work well in the morning," Grandpa said, as he tied the fly onto the thin leader. Completing the knot, he set the hook in the cork handle of the fly rod before passing the rod to me and preparing his own rod for our morning adventure.

The afternoon before, we had stood in the large grassy meadow down the hill in front of the cabin and practiced casting a fly rod. Placing the rod in my hand, Grandpa had demonstrated how to cast the long rod and how to handle fly line by drawing the line from the reel and pulling the line out and away from my body while at the same time keeping the butt of the rod held tight in my right hand. After having pulled enough of the thick yellow-brown line from the red automatic Martin reel, Grandpa took hold of the rod and demonstrated how to cast the strange, thick line by raising the pole up and to the right of him and waving it back and forth, pushing more and more line through the eyelets toward his target with each forward swing of the rod. I watched enthusiastically the ease with which the line shot forward from the tip of the pole and delicately unfurled itself into a straight line onto the grass in front of us.

As he handed the rod back to me, Grandpa positioned my arm to mimic his own, to show me how to begin the casting motion. He helped me as I waved my arm forward and back—slowly at first, so that I could get the feel for the weight of the rod and what its action felt like as it cut through the air in front of and behind me to the point where the rod tip stopped over my right shoulder. "Now you give it a try," Grandpa directed me, after pressing the lever on the red Martin reel to draw in most of the line that he had so gracefully cast across the meadow only minutes before. With all the might of an eight-year-old little boy, I whipped the pole to and fro past my right ear listening to the rod cut the air as Grandpa stood off to the side and watched. "No, no, no, you're trying to cast too quickly," he told me in his stern, reassuring voice. He directed me to pull the handle of the reel and take in a bit more of the line, then try again.

It's hard now to remember how much time went by with the two of us in the meadow working the fly rod while the sun passed through the tops of the lodgepole pines around us. The chattering squirrels were clearly unimpressed, as they skittered up and down the surrounding trees, all the while castigating my clumsy efforts from atop woody branches. Eventually I began to get the rhythm required to pass the mass of line I had drawn off the reel through the eyes of the fly rod to fall to the ground in a heap somewhere in front of me, and I finally succeeded in making the line go from a tangled mess at my feet to a tangled mess on the grass in front of us. Grandpa assured me that this was quite all right. As the afternoon's lesson drew to a close, I noticed that the line had begun to make a snapping sound as it unfurled in the air behind me just prior to beginning its rapid journey forward to the meadow grass in front of us. Somehow I knew the line shouldn't snap like that. When I asked about it, Grandpa responded, "Don't worry about that too much right now. It will happen less once leader and a fly have been tied on."

Come the next morning, I had lost nearly all the skills I had obtained during the previous afternoon's lesson. My attention shifted from being trans-fixed by the small black fly hooked into the cork on my rod to dwelling on how chilly it was while watching my breath hang in the air around me. The chill was expelled from my mind and my body, though, as we walked down the path to the stream. At the bottom of the trail, we turned to the left, and Grandpa led the way down a second, much less worn trail that paralleled the stream. I followed close behind, stepping over fallen logs, many of which had been on the ground so long that when I accidently tripped over them, they burst in a silent explosion of orange and red spongy wood. The forest around us was painted in a muted gray that rested atop the early morning dark greens of trees, shrubs, and willows.

Only our voices broke the early morning's stillness as we made our way along the trail. Even the stream itself seemed to be covered by a blanket of sleepy muteness, babbling quietly in the background. "Grandma's favorite places to fish are upstream here," Grandpa told me, as we made our way toward our destination, an area where the water was saturated in darkness as large subalpine firs closed in precariously near each side of the stream bank.

A large, flat boulder not far from the bank protruded from the shadowed waters, free of branches from the many nearby trees. Grandpa stepped onto the boulder and then watched closely as I made a short hop from the stream-bank to the rock. The dew-wet soles of my worn and dingy shoes didn't in-stantly grip the dry surface of the rock, and my pole waved wildly in my hand as I sought to catch my balance until Grandpa reached out to steady me. With a knowing eye, he scanned the dark water that stretched from the rock toward the opposite bank and then looked downstream, glancing up occasionally to take the measure of the evergreen branches overhanging the stream.

With a nod, he turned to me. "OK, unhook your fly and let it drop in the water here," he said, motioning to the front of the rock whose edge pointed directly downstream. "Now, pull out some line like I showed you." I pulled the thick yellow-brown line from the Martin automatic reel until told "enough." Pointing to the water between the rock and the far bank, Grandpa said, "Take a practice cast out over here, but be careful of the trees." I took a slow step toward that side of the boulder and brought the fly rod straight up in front of me. Seeing my hesitation to begin casting, he stepped from behind me and placed his hand over mine, helping me cast the line I'd drawn out. He watched intently until my confidence had grown enough to cast the line on my own. So intent was I on making an adequate cast that I'd forgotten a fly was attached to the end of the line with the intent to catch a fish.

"OK, Brad, now I want you to try and cast your line at an angle and let the fly float downstream until it reaches that pool on the edge of the bank." My gaze followed the water from the downstream edge of the rock on which we were standing, and I saw the slow water of the deep pool near the bank downstream from us that Grandpa had pointed toward. Only a short time earlier we had walked by that very spot on our way to the rock. I flailed the water in front of me with the fly line, watching as it landed in the water in front of us like a tangled pile of overcooked spaghetti. The moderate current grabbed the line slowly at first and tugged at it, unwinding the mess I had made into a relatively straight line leading from the eye at the top of my rod to the fly at the far end of the line. The little black gnat at the end of my line bounced on top of the water's surface, as the current beneath it flowed on, uninterrupted by my antics.

"Move the tip of your rod slightly to the right," Grandpa instructed, as we both watched the little fly skitter across the water's dark surface. I did as I was told, and the black gnat responded by settling back down into the water and drifting slowly into the calmer waters of the dark pool beneath the tree.

After a little while, he had me draw the line back in and cast again. As we went through the process, the morning grays began to soften, and sunlight lightly kissed the tops of the trees on the west side of the forested ridges above us, but my attention was almost completely focused on the little black gnat as it made its short journey from swift water to slow water to the water at my feet, and then back again.

Finally, during one of these journeys, I suddenly saw the water around it burble and the fly disappear. Just as suddenly the rod in my hand jumped to life as the fish that had taken my black gnat tugged at the other end. I immediately yelled, "What do I do?" Calmly, Grandpa told me to pull the tip of the rod up and toward me, then pull the lever on the reel. As I brought the rod toward me, I felt the fish on the other end resist my effort to reel him in. My heart was ready to burst with excitement!

I pulled on the lever and the gears inside the reel spun and quickly drew the line toward me and onto the spool of the reel. As the reel pulled the fish toward the boulder, I felt the tug-of-war taking place between the fish at the end of my line and the gears of the reel. The Martin reel whirred as it quickly pulled the line off the water, but I could tell the fish was fighting back when the whir of the gears slowed ever so slightly and elongated. In a few moments, though, the fish that had been fooled by the little black gnat was splashing in the water at the base of our rock. Reaching down, Grandpa quickly scooped it from the water and, with one swift motion, worked the hook loose from the corner of its lip and handed the squirming beauty to me.

It was cold, slimy, and very much alive. But more than that, it was a specimen of beauty. It was a tiny brook trout, but as far as I was concerned, it was as noble as any marlin mounted on any wall. My young eyes were immediately drawn to the sight of the shining white belly contrasted against the dark green of its flanks. Within that dark green, little red spots were surrounded by halos of blue. This entire color palette was located below an even darker green along the fish's back, and that dark green had small lighter green squiggles within it (I would later learn that these were called vermiculations). Its little fins went from green, to orange, to white at the tips. How, I wondered, did such a colorful fish stay so easily unseen to the naked eye?

My amazement was cut short when Grandpa told me to place the fish back in the water, since it was too small to keep. There was a six-inch size limit on brook trout in the stream, and this one hardly met the requirement. With no small amount of regret, I squatted down and placed my hand in the water at the edge of the boulder that protruded farthest into the stream. When I opened my hand, my catch darted through my fingers into the cold water. I looked on for a few moments before standing up, not sure what to do next. Seeing childish uncertainty again written across my face, Grandpa smiled and told me, "Well, let's try for another. How about a bigger one this time? If we don't catch another here, we will head upstream." I could feel the smile stretching across my face as I pulled line from the reel and prepared to cast, ready to begin punishing the water again with my tangled spaghetti line.

CHAPTER 4

Freedom to Roam

I HAVE COME TO BELIEVE that growing up poor allowed for a childhood freedom that more than made up for what it denied me in terms of other types of opportunities. The hard times we endured also sharpened the fun that we did have, in the same way that hunger makes the smell of food from the kitchen all the more tempting. And one of the great benefits to being part of a large family was that there was always action, movement, activity.

The press of so many children in such a small house made our yearning for the outdoors that much greater, and it was a yearning our parents actively encouraged. If the temperature and weather were decent and we had not already made our way outside, we would be ordered out and given explicit instructions to not come back in until mealtime. What child wouldn't think this a ticket for full-on, unadulterated fun? We made the most of it: if solitary games of imagination became boring, there were enough of us to develop some sort of team game, whether a known sport or some made-up-on-the-spot game with ad hoc rules decided on by committee. Either way, the outcome was likely a good time for all of us—with a few scuffles and bloody noses thrown in.

RIVER HIJINKS

When not playing with my siblings, I would often poke my head in the front door of the trailer to announce that I was "going down to the river." I would wait the requisite one second to see whether a sharp "No" was forthcoming;

if not, I would leave quickly and slip down the steep, unvegetated hill behind the house to the banks of the Shoshone River just below the trailer park.

I was just as likely to run down to the river to play as I was to fish. The portion of the Shoshone near home never called to me in the same way as the river's headwaters that descended the Absaroka Mountains west of Cody. Much of the summertime flow was pulled from the river to irrigate immense fields of sugar beets, beans, and barley, and the runoff that was returned from the fields was warm and filled with chemicals. During the agricultural season, the river was filled with sediment and fertilizer, which turned it a sickly rotten-flesh green. The banks were filled with weeds of every sort that had been flushed downstream and with non-native Russian olive trees that had spines protruding from branch and bole, waiting to tear clothes or spear exposed skin. If I decided to carry a pole down to the river with me, I could occasionally catch a trout if patience and luck both ran the right direction, but trout were the species least likely to be caught. The thick, churning waters flowing near town were far more likely to be inhabited by chubs, suckers, and carp, all of which were considered trash fish by most people in the community.

The freedom we were given allowed me to roam the nearby countryside as far as my feet or bike would carry me. Occasionally, the oldest of us would band together to go swimming in the river during the summer. Childhood bravado takes on a whole new meaning when you're attempting to outdare your stepsiblings. One memorable incident occurred when several of us had joined up with some of my middle school friends to swim in the river (I suspect had my friends' parents known we were swimming in the Shoshone River unsupervised, those friends wouldn't have been allowed over to my house anymore). The goal of the day's game became to find the most difficult place to swim across the river. We walked upstream a short distance from the two-lane bridge that crossed the river as the road headed into Byron and decided that the rough water that poured from the bend would be a great place to test our mettle.

I don't remember who was the first to try to swim across and was swept downstream to the shallower waters. What I do remember with vivid clarity is my first attempt at crossing. I waded out up to my waist, then jumped forward. I was immediately caught by the current, which I had expected; what I wasn't prepared for was being pulled under. The world darkened as the water closed in over my head, and then my feet hit the bottom of the riverbed. Right at that moment, I remember seeing in my mind a newspaper article titled "Local Boy Drowns in River."

I can't remember the next few moments with the clarity that I remember the preceding seconds, but my head quickly broke the surface of the water. I am sure I swam with all the strength I had in my bird-like arms, as the current continued to sweep me downstream. Wading back on shore, shaking, I told my friends about getting pulled under and of the vision of the headline I'd had. Despite my scare, and along with some laughs and a little friendly ribbing, we all tried our hand at challenging the river several more times that day.

BOYS ON THEIR OWN

Around the same time as my semitraumatic incident down at the river, my parents bought a second trailer-house that had been put up for sale after one of our next-door neighbors passed away. The "new" trailer-house gave us two additional bedrooms, which were allocated to the four oldest boys (there was only about eighteen months' difference between the four of us).

Every night when sent to bed, we left the trailer that my parents and youngest siblings lived in and walked the short distance over to the second trailer. Yes, four teenage boys were allowed to spend each and every night largely unsupervised. Instead of running wild until the cops showed up at the door with me in hand, I only occasionally walked out the back door of the trailer in the dark of night to stroll around town or partake in other mischief. Even when I had friends over, we were mostly content to huddle in my bedroom and play Dungeons & Dragons.

Although being trusted to live our nights largely unsupervised was tremendous fun, winter was a trying time. We were required to turn the furnace thermostat down to the absolute minimum before we left for school and not allowed to turn it back up again until just before bedtime. During the first winter this hardly bothered me at all. Heck, I was a teen almost allowed to live on his own—so what if I had to wear a coat in the place until bedtime? In retrospect, I think my parents may have done that purposely as a way to keep us next door and therefore limit the amount of trouble we could get into.

The immense freedom that accompanied living in a separate trailer-house from my parents reduced the shame I felt over our poverty. But that shame stabbed home again one day at school when I was pulling my friends together to see if they wanted to stay one night that weekend to play Dungeons & Dragons. One of my friends who regularly joined our gaming group turned to me in the hall and said matter-of-factly, "I don't like going to your house. It's too cold." The revelation stunned me, and I was left wondering how many of my friends felt that way. Fortunately, the fun and friendship outweighed the cold of my bedroom, though, since a core group of friends was happy to come over at every available opportunity.

EXISTENTIAL FREEDOM

As long as my chores were completed, I was allowed tremendous latitude to decide what to do with my time and where to go. During winter, after spending an hour cutting firewood with a handsaw after school, my time was largely my own, and I relished it. It didn't matter whether I was playing outside, reading, or writing adventures for our next role-playing game get-together—the time was my own, as was the space. From the riverbanks below the house to the school playground across the street to dirt roads beyond town that I explored on my bike, I was allowed to roam to my heart's content.

But no amount of freedom from our cramped trailer-house existence would ever compare to the existential freedom that I found at the cabin. "Existential freedom" may seem like a bit of hyperbole, but I don't think it is. My time at the cabin created opportunities for me to discover life on my own terms, and my experiences fly fishing there opened the world to me in ways that deeply connected me to nature and sharpened my desire to explore the world. I found beauty in trout, complexity in water, and challenges in the vegetation that grew alongside the stream. After catching my first fish with

Grandpa that chilly morning, I felt increasingly called to explore my world. The rewards I have reaped from this call to the water have shaped my life. Two events, in particular, can perhaps clarify why I think of this freedom as existential: the day I got my first fly rod and the day I discovered the rock island on the stream below the cabin.

I was ten the summer the Johnson family reunion was held at the family cabin. Brandon and I arrived with our grandparents earlier than the rest of the family, in order to get the cabin prepared for our aunts, uncles, cousins, second cousins, and long-lost family, as well as the myriad friends who would fill the cabin to overflowing. With so many guests, beds quickly became scarce, and sleeping bags became the order of the day for the younger members of the family. I spent most nights of the reunion in a nylon pup tent pitched on bare ground beneath the pines that filled the small hill between the cabin and the stream. At night the rush of the creek in the darkness lulled me to sleep with thoughts of tomorrow's trout jumping in my head.

It was the first summer that I fished with a fly rod that I owned myself. In anticipation of cabin trips to come that summer, Grandma and Grandpa had taken me to the sporting-goods shop in town and bought the rod and reel combo for me. It was a brown-and-yellow Eagle Claw fiberglass combination fly/spin rod that broke down into four pieces and came with its own yellow sleeve to protect it inside an oversized silver aluminum tube. The rod was stiff and if I cast too often without checking the fit of the ferrules, it would disconnect midcast, sending the top half of the rod into the stream to be retrieved by my reeling in the line while hoping that the fly would catch the eyelet; if it didn't, I would be forced to run down the bank and jump in the water to retrieve the missing piece. I struggled with casting. My technique largely consisted of flinging the line onto the water, then pulling it back off to cast, rather than keeping the line elevated above my head with false casts until I was ready to present the fly on the water. In my mind, though, my casting had improved considerably since that first afternoon a couple of years earlier in the meadow below the cabin.

It was the summer that my fly fishing explorations took off in earnest. My initial explorations of the creek below Rubyat had taken me weaving through trees and over rotting logs on my way upstream along the same footpaths that my grandfather and I had followed whenever I had accompanied him fishing. The summer of the Johnson family reunion, with my brand new rod in hand, I was ready to explore new lands. Instead of heading upstream at the bottom of the path, I turned my soggy tennis shoes downstream.

It was July and, as usual for that time of year, the flow of Tensleep Creek was low enough for me to safely wade the stream, which meant more opportunities to cast to trout in the remaining pools and beneath revealed undercut banks. I shuffled slowly along exposed cobble in the stream just beyond the island that rested within a couple of arm's lengths from the bank where the path from the cabin terminated. My goal was to cast my fly underneath the branches of the willow that reached out over the western bank. I had never cast a fly along that portion of the stream before, due to the volume of willows that were arrayed along the bank, but I had determined that today was going to be different. Just beyond the willows, the stream narrowed as it turned and flowed into a short bend. The water was too deep and swift for me to attempt to wade farther downstream, so I carefully strode toward shore and pulled myself out of the stream by grabbing hold of the willows I'd just been casting beneath. Raising my shiny new fly rod in front of me like a knight's salute, I pushed through the tangle of branches until, stumbling out of the willows, I found myself in the shadow of familiar lodgepole pines with the cabin on the hill just above me.

Looking back at the willows I had just fought my way through, I followed their unbroken wall of vegetation with my eye. I yearned to discover what secrets the waters held just below where I had been casting, but the tangled maze of willows was unassailable. I turned and slowly stalked beneath the pine trees until I found an opening between the willows and pines that revealed the meadow that I knew so well from the vantage point of the porch swing. I charged off, fly rod and creel in hand, across the meadow in search of the nearby stream.

It was only a short distance that I covered, but in my mind, I was exploring a new continent. The mountain stream remained elusive, hidden behind streamside willows, but the sound of the creek nearby continued to call to me.

Unable to find an opening that led directly to the stream, I decided to push my way through the willows in the same manner as when I had left the stream a few minutes earlier. Again brandishing my fly rod before me, I pushed my way into a stand of willows that towered well over my head, threading my feet over and around the roots that thrust out of the dark, water-filled holes in which the willows had found a home. More than once I had to turn around when I found a hole too deep with water to safely jump across, but with adolescent determination I pushed on.

My determination was rewarded when a shove of branches found me perched precariously on a small patch of grass overlooking the deepest hole in the stream I had ever seen. Looking upstream, I realized that I was now at the tail end of the short bend in the stream I had left behind. As I turned to look the other direction, I saw, to my amazement, a massive island composed of small cobblestone river rock. On three sides of the island, the water was deep and inviting. The shallowest water was nearest to where I was standing, just downstream, but I would have to again fight my way through the willows to get there. Now fully in exploration mode, I found my way to the shallower water through the willow thicket and jumped from the willow-covered undercut bank into the narrow channel separating me from the rock island.

Beautiful waters ran on two sides of the island where the narrow stream-flow had cut deep troughs. On the tail end of the island, where the majority of the water came together again, a set of riffles spread from bank to bank before entering a shallow and smooth run that then turned into a wide bend. At a distance east of me was a beaver dam. For the next few years, the dam and the waters behind it would be beyond my reach, since the waters leading to it were too deep for me to safely cross.

Discovering the rock island was a seminal event for me, as the island would become the central focus of my fishing exploits for the next several years. The gift of my first fly rod from my grandparents, along with the discovery of the rock island, cemented my connection to this piece of land and these waters. It also cemented my place in family lore during the family reunion, due to the considerable amount of time I spent on the water and the prodigious amount of trout that I brought back up to the cabin each day. I filled my creel limit on several days, returning to the cabin with the trout cleaned and ready for the frying pan—morning, afternoon, and evening. Often, even after I reached my limit, and encouraged by the family accolades, I would return to the stream and spend more hours releasing trout back into the stream as quickly as I caught them.

One afternoon that summer, while standing on the northern edge of the rock island, embraced by the warmth of a mountain summer afternoon, I decided to tie two flies on my leader. Ignoring the squish of my wet tennis shoes as I squatted down, I first tied one of my favorite flies, a royal coachman, which rather than replicating an actual insect, was an artful conglomeration of feathers, hair, and thread intended to stimulate trout to strike based on the flash of colors and shape. Below this I tied a black gnat, the same fly that I had used when I caught my first fish with Grandpa only a few summers prior.

Stepping to the edge of the island, I looked closely into the deep pool, wondering what species of trout I would find hidden in its depths. I quickly scanned the branches of the willows overhanging the edge of the bank closest to me, noting that a few branches dipped into the stream, causing the water to rush past and breaking up the otherwise still surface of the pool. Following a few water-slapping casts on the surface of the pool, I quickly stripped in the slack bright-green line as it floated toward me. My reward was a four-inch brook trout caught nearly at my feet . . . not quite what I had expected.

I again flailed the water, this time casting as close as I could to the willows dipping into the water near the edge of the pool, hoping that the disturbance caused by the shrub's soggy branches might be somewhere a trout would find enticing on a hot summer day. My ten-year-old logic worked. As I again stripped the line in, I was stopped by a sudden tension in the line; a fish was at the other end, and it was big enough that I didn't throw it at my feet as I vigorously stripped the line toward me. In an exuberant overreaction, I dropped the line in my left hand and began to reel with my right. The trout on the other end sensed its opening and darted upstream (thankfully, since if it had headed downstream, it could have used the slack line to its advantage). I danced up and down the small rocky point, reeling excitedly, trying to reestablish tension in the line. Luck was with me as the trout shot upstream to the upper end of the pool, moving away from the potentially tangling willows. The fish on the other end of my line refused to reveal itself, instead staying hidden in the dark water. As I slowly managed to reel in my line, the clear monofilament leader became visible at the surface of the water. I lifted the tip of my stiff Eagle Claw rod high over my head and walked backward, determined to not let the unseen trout escape as a result of poor handling at the very end of our fight. When I finally pulled the trout from the water, I found an eight-inch brook trout had taken the gaudy royal coachman. But the true surprise came when I pulled in the remainder of my leader from the water: a second brook trout, half the size of the first (OK, maybe it was only three inches . . .), had taken the black gnat!

I couldn't believe it: I had done what I had always been told was only an empty boast made up by fishermen returning from the river skunked. I had caught two fish on the same cast! A few years later in seventh-grade shop class, I would sit and listen as the teacher—a kindly and industrious man who understood how to shape pupils as well as wood—told the class that anyone who said they had caught two fish on the same cast was a liar. I knew better than to say anything, but I also knew the truth. Two flies are better than one . . . and stocked brook trout are gullible.

Brook trout were not the only species of trout I pulled from the complex waters surrounding the rock island. Rainbow trout were plentiful, and I learned that large and aggressive brown trout could be lured from beneath cut banks and logs, if I could only make the cast. The rock island was generous with its piscine bounty for as long as I was willing to ply my trade along its cobbles. Of course, what I didn't realize at the time was that none of the fish I caught there were native to my beloved waters below the cabin.

CHAPTER 5

A Personal Debt to Theodore Roosevelt

I HAVE LONG BEEN AN admirer of Theodore Roosevelt, but it was only recently that I realized the personal debt of gratitude that I owed him. Roosevelt's political acumen, scientific and conservation efforts, and ability as an author are all well known. As a statesman, he was as comfortable giving speeches along dusty territorial roads as he was rubbing elbows with the European aristocracy. As a sportsman, his exploits were almost legendary during his lifetime and have diminished little in reputation since. There has yet to be an individual in the modern era who has ascended to such heights and can boast of such broad accomplishments.

Our great American public land system, while imperfect, owes much of its current configuration to the vision and idealism of our twenty-sixth president. The case could be made that all Americans owe him a tremendous debt of gratitude for his progressive views on natural resource policies, which resulted in the creation of our vast national forests and wildlife refuges, not to mention the national monuments and national parks that would eventually follow.[2] Roosevelt has been applauded for his efforts to conserve America's wildlife, forests, and waters, both within or outside the public domain. His record shows that he recognized that resource development was a component of natural resource conservation and that he attempted to strike a balance between the two sides of natural resource management.[3]

The battle between development and conservation of natural resources has raged since the inception of the public domain. A pivotal moment in the debate over public lands came with the U.S. Census Bureau's 1890 announcement that the American frontier had closed.[4] That year the Census Bureau determined that the interior of the United States had been settled to such an extent that a wilderness frontier was no longer discernible. The closing of the frontier drove home the realization that the United States—its lands and its resources—were indeed finite, which led to a wider understanding of the need to conserve the country's natural resources, including those found within the public domain.

Despite the closing of the American frontier and the corresponding impact it had on the American psyche, federal ownership, management, development, and ultimately conservation of natural resources continued to prove contentious. Many of the frontier territories west of the Mississippi River that were admitted to the Union following the Civil War were required, as part of their enabling charter, to relinquish any presumed rights to federal public lands within their borders. What this meant in practice was that a new state's ability to exploit a considerable amount of the natural resources within its borders, such as timber and minerals, was constrained by the need to first seek federal approval. The result has been a lengthy history of condemnation, and sometimes outright hatred, of the federal government for an arrangement that many have proclaimed to be a form of modern-day colonialism in which western states are subjugated to the federal government. Some view the arrangement as preventing the western states from being free, as their eastern sister states have been, to develop their natural resources as they see fit, thereby denying western states control of their own destiny.[5] In recent years, the perception of federal government malfeasance through public land policy has resulted in attempts by state legislatures to wrest control of federal public lands from the federal government or to nullify federal laws through state or local legislation.[6] But this is not the first time that western states have attempted to gain control: the Sagebrush Rebellion of the late 1970s, the County Supremacy Movement of the 1980s, and the Wise Use Movement of the 1990s each sought, in some form and to varying degrees, to wrest control of public lands away from the federal government and into the hands of the state or the county.

Theodore Roosevelt recognized the need to conserve and manage the resources found on public lands for the long-term benefit of future generations, which did not preclude development of those resources. And as is always the case with far-reaching and controversial policies, his vision of public land management did not go unchallenged and may well have been as equally disliked as it was appreciated.[7] But Roosevelt was never one to let the negative opinions of others sway his decision-making. He was consistently decisive about public land policy, and the echoes of his values, policies, and choices can still be heard in our current debates over public land management.

ROOSEVELT, THE SPORTSMAN

Roosevelt's outdoor exploits were well recorded by his own pen, as well as in the work of historians. In August 1884, at age twenty-five and already a widower, he left his ranch in North Dakota for the Bighorn Mountains of Wyoming in pursuit of the largest carnivore in the lower forty-eight states: the grizzly bear. The trip followed the death of his young wife, Alice, and of his mother on the same fateful evening of February 14 earlier that year, with his wife succumbing to Bright's disease, and his mother to typhus.[8] Alice had given birth to their only child just two days before her death. Roosevelt sought solace for his decimated soul and broken heart at his Maltese Cross ranch in the Badlands of North Dakota. It was from this ranch that he departed for his trip to the Bighorn Mountains, which he documented in *Hunting Trips of a Ranchman*, first published in 1885, and also referenced in a later book, *The Wilderness Hunter*, published in 1893.

The Bighorn Mountains in which I grew up fly fishing, hiking, and camping are still home to bears, although not the grizzly bears that Roosevelt sought. Today, the black bear—the smaller and less aggressive cousin to Roosevelt's quarry—roams the Bighorn Mountains. When Roosevelt sought out Old Ephraim (as he called the grizzly) in 1884, the Bighorns were still very much a wilderness mountain chain in the sparsely populated Wyoming

Territory. Today, the Bighorn Mountains are an "island" mountain chain, surrounded by a sagebrush steppe and prairie sea that is home to heavy industrialization. The only expanse of this former frontier where the impacts of man are not clearly etched on the landscape are the parts within the Cloud Peak Wilderness area.

Roosevelt's grizzly bear tally during the hunting trip reflects a wilderness ecosystem not yet fragmented or heavily disturbed. He and his guide, Bill Merrifield, whom he had initially hired in 1883 to assist in managing his cattle operation in North Dakota, together shot several grizzly bears, an accomplishment Roosevelt described succinctly in *Hunting Trips of a Ranchman*: "While on this trip we killed five grizzlies with seven bullets." Their hunting exploits on that trip also encompassed elk, white-tail and black-tail deer, various forms of rabbit, and a plethora of bird species, including both blue grouse and sage-grouse.[9]

While Theodore Roosevelt's love for hunting and his extraordinary hunting tallies are legendary among sportsmen, he was not, much to my disappointment, a dedicated fly fisherman. An article by Western and fly fishing historian Paul Schullery written for the American Museum of Fly Fishing makes a strong case that while Theodore Roosevelt did fish, including fly fish, he was not an avid fisherman, regardless of the type of tackle.[10] Instead Roosevelt's passion was for the more strenuous activity of hunting, with a particular preference for big game hunting.

Schullery notes that even though fishing was not a focal point of Roosevelt's outdoor life, he would engage in it as a means of sustenance during outdoor adventures. On their way to the Bighorn Mountains in pursuit of grizzly bears, for example, Roosevelt and Merrifield caught fifty trout on September 11, 1884. Giving credence to Roosevelt's ability to turn any activity into a strenuous affair, the two men again pursued trout a week later, on September 19, this time walking and climbing into a steep-sided, boulder-covered valley to get to a lake containing "spotted trout." Using dead cedar branches as poles, the men quickly found that the "ravenous" trout were easily caught even on makeshift gear and provided an easy and delectable meal.[11] This excursion was not the only time Roosevelt improvised equipment in order to fish; Schullery, quoting Roosevelt as a teenager, notes that he even used a gun barrel to "do duty as a fishing rod."[12]

Clearly, Roosevelt made the most out of the fishing opportunities in which he chose to engage. In recognition of Roosevelt's outdoor and scientific exploits and in honor of his commissioning of the survey of the Kern River drainage that is home to the golden trout, the golden trout found in Volcano Creek of California's Sierra Nevada were, for a time, recognized taxonomically as *Salmo rooseveli* (eventually, based on the work of Robert Behnke, these trout were recognized as part of the South Fork Kern River subspecies and reclassified as *Oncorhynchus mykiss aguabonita*).[13]

A STRENUOUS LIFE

While I feel a connection to Roosevelt's adventures in the Bighorn Mountains and his vision of natural resource conservation, the greatest debt I owe him is for his advancement of the idea of the "strenuous life." The young Theodore Roosevelt was sickly as a child and, prompted in part by his father, set out to physically overcome his weaknesses. Through grueling physical training and outdoor adventure, he developed strength and physical stamina that helped diminish, although not totally relieve, his childhood illnesses.[14] After setting this physically challenging course for himself early in life, he continued, throughout the remainder of his life, to advocate and partake in grueling outdoor activity and to promote this type of activity publicly as the "strenuous life."

While Roosevelt's physically demanding outdoor regimen originated in his childhood frailty, he would eventually come to see the strenuous lifestyle as a means of overcoming what he believed was a weakening of American society, both physically and socially, as a result of urban living.[15] My great-great-grandfather Ruby Shultz lived during this era, and while I have no way of knowing whether he was a disciple of Roosevelt's strenuous life, I have no doubt that he embodied it.

The Term Occupancy Act passed by Congress in 1915 was the enabling legislation that allowed my great-great-grandfather to pursue his particular version of a strenuous life. The act allowed private citizens the opportunity to lease land from the Forest Service, which a home or cabin could then be built upon. During the summer of 1916, Ruby Shultz, along with a number of like-minded friends from in and around Worland, Wyoming, went up into the Bighorn Mountains and began felling lodgepole pines and assembling them into what would become Rubyat. The work was arduous and long—in fact, long enough that construction of the three-room cabin would not be complete until the summer of 1917.

Ruby Shultz was a many-faceted individual, to say the least. In addition to avidly pursuing outdoor recreation, he painted landscapes and had a particular passion for mountain scenes. He is also famous within the family for watercolor works that were painted over the top of black-and-white photos. His professional life was as a pharmacist in Worland, and there are still treasured mementos of his trade to be found among the shelves of the cabin: old empty bottles, tiny and large, with labels that transport the observer back to a time when medicine and its application were dramatically different.

Human activity in the Bighorn Mountains has changed dramatically in the century since Ruby built the cabin. In the early days of the cabin, when cars themselves were still in their youth, the road to the cabin was a rutted and rock-filled, muffler- and oil-pan-eating, two-track forest road. Utility, rather than convenience, was the motivation for the road design of the era. My cousin Johanna remembers the condition of the road being so poor that her mother warned her not to talk to her father while they traversed it. Today, the main thoroughfare up to West Tensleep Lake is a wide and well-maintained road that allows vehicles to zoom up the valley. Likewise, the character of the forest's flora and fauna has changed. My grandfather remembers deer being more plentiful in the past and not seeing any moose until twenty to twenty-five years ago—which is to say, only in my lifetime have moose become common around the family cabin.

The use of the land and waters of the Bighorn Mountains has evolved, as well. The older generations of my family remember when livestock grazing, including both cattle and sheep, was allowed all over the mountain valley. Of course, wherever livestock grazing is allowed, predators are not appreciated and, in many cases, simply are not tolerated. The Bighorn Mountains are no different in this respect than the Great Plains, where trapping and poisoning were used to reduce or completely remove predators from the landscape for the benefit of livestock production. Nevertheless, the quiet and elusive mountain lion has held on in the Bighorn Mountains, and several members of my family have seen one contemplating the benefits of a free-range livestock meal.

I heard one such story in Cody, Wyoming, at the home of my cousin Tom Shultz and his wife, Cheryl. During the years when livestock grazing was still prevalent in the area, Tom had been walking along a trail that at times parallels Willow Creek, a smaller creek that runs near Tensleep Creek. As he made his way down the trail, Tom discovered a large logjam on the creek, likely the result of the high flows from that year's spring runoff. A movement from atop the logjam caught his eye: hanging from the piled logs, a long muted-gold tail lazily swept back and forth. After watching the tail for a moment, he lifted his gaze to find the tail attached to a tawny and muscular mountain lion. At the same moment, he became aware of the bleating of sheep on the opposite side of the logjam, as a herd meandered slowly downstream. More movement caught Tom's eye, this time from the base of the logjam: a second mountain lion was crouched at the base of the wooden barricade, coiled like a spring. In one graceful motion, the second lion easily unwound its honed muscles, propelling itself to the top of the log pile, where it joined its companion in overlooking the wool-covered potential smorgasbord.

A FAMILY PURSUIT

Even though the character of the stream that runs past the cabin has changed since Ruby began construction of the cabin in 1916, one constant is that the art of fly fishing has continually been pursued upon it. Just as I was a student of my grandfather, so he was a student of his. One sunny afternoon in Worland, Wyoming, while sitting at the kitchen table where I had enjoyed so many meals as a child, my grandfather imparted to me that fly fishing was a pursuit that our family had already followed for many generations. He told me that his grandfather Ruby believed "there was only one proper way of catching a trout and that was on a dry fly." That single quote embodies for me the familial roots of my passion for fly fishing.

Like so much else, the character of the fish that my family has pursued on the stream has changed over time, as the trout that inhabit the stream have been manipulated according to man's desire for a particular quarry. The Yellowstone cutthroat trout is the trout native to the waters of the Bighorn Mountains, the same trout that is native to the water of the Yellowstone River from which the species takes its name. And while you can find a few remnant populations of the subspecies in the Bighorn Mountains, the natives are no longer found in the stream that runs below Rubyat.

While I was interviewing my grandfather for this book, he told me he had no recollection of catching the cutthroat trout native to Tensleep Creek, but he did remember that when he was a child of ten years old or so, some adults had talked about having caught them. I don't know if people were still catching the native trout in the stream below the cabin at that time or if they were simply talking about having caught them during years past. No matter how you parse it, though, the trout native to the stream have long been absent.

The cabin was originally only three interior rooms: a kitchen, great room, and bedroom; the front porch that stretches from the front door along two sides of the cabin was not part of the original build. If you walk around the sides of the porch and cast your gaze from wooden-slat floor to planked interior roof, you will observe a difference between each side in the cut and texture of the wood that was used, evidence of one having followed the other in time and materials. The tongue-and-groove flooring for the porch was largely obtained from the sawmill at Bear Lake, just up the road from the cabin. The sawmill has long since disappeared, but remnants of its history remain. The first cabin that you pass along the narrow two-track spur road leading to Rubyat is believed to have once served as the dining hall for the sawmill workers. I can envision the mill workers traipsing down the hillside from the sawmill for a hot lunch at long wooden tables inside the log cabin, then grabbing a communal fly rod to slip the few additional yards down to the stream to take a few casts, perhaps pulling a little brook trout from the creek before returning to finish out the afternoon shift.

My great-great-grandfather left his personal impression on the cabin, from top to bottom. For me, the most visible artifact he left for the family, other than the cabin itself, is a massive face carved from a burl and hung on the outside western wall of the cabin. The burl is a twisted and knotted growth from the side of a local tree trunk; I'm told that the tree from which this burl was harvested nearly a century ago was found near Willow Creek on the far side of the stream below the cabin. Putting his creative mind and wood-working talents to the test, my great-great-grandfather carved from that three-foot-diameter twisted knot of wood a smiling face with a full set of teeth that would have done Theodore Roosevelt proud. He attached a Jimmy Durante–like nose to the face using a barkless, hooked limb and then completed the carving by attaching small pine-branch eyebrows. That smiling face beams down on everyone who makes the trip to the cabin and, in its wooden grin, encompasses the joy that is found while visiting Rubyat.

Theodore Roosevelt's progressive natural resource policies and his extolling of the strenuous life surely set the stage for my great-great-grandfather's vision and realization of a family cabin in the Bighorn Mountains of Wyoming. And while Roosevelt wasn't known for his fly fishing enthusiasm, it is possible that I have fished some of the same waters he did during his trip to the Bighorn Mountains in search of grizzly bears in 1884. Along with the cabin, Ruby Shultz passed down to future generations of my family a love of the sport of fly fishing and, through it, a connection to the natural world. The fauna of the streams and forest, as well as the character of the Bighorn Mountains, have changed dramatically since the days of Theodore Roosevelt and my great-great-grandfather, but even an ephemeral connection to such a rich history is worth cherishing.

CHAPTER 6

Forgotten Waters

TWO YEARS AFTER MY DISCOVERY of the rock island, my grandmother died of a cancer I hadn't even known she had, and my trips to the cabin came to an abrupt end. The loss of my grandmother meant the loss of my childhood refuge as well. The discordance of this period of my life was made worse by my transition from middle school to high school, an awkward time for most teenagers and one made worse for me by a heightened sense of my own nerdiness. My feelings of loss from my grandmother's passing and the cessation of weekend and summer trips to my grandparents' house were diffused, however, as my adolescent thoughts and interests shifted.

As my connection to the cabin and my home-waters faded, my interest in fly fishing waned but was never extinguished. The need for game meat to feed the family had grown in tandem with the increased appetites of seven growing children. During these years, family fishing trips to local waters were still a common outing. All nine of us would somehow pile into our 1970s faux-wood-paneled Oldsmobile, with its two rows of backseats—a car that had once belonged to my maternal grandfather. The bickering that was common in the confines of a trailer-house was amplified as we drove to our destination.

Yellowtail Reservoir, which had been filled by the damming of the Bighorn River in Montana in the 1960s, was one of my parents' favorite fishing destinations. Leaving the highway behind, we would drive past the eerie Kane Cemetery, one of the last remnants of the town of Kane that had been flooded as the Yellowtail Reservoir was filled to capacity for the first time.

Trees and scrub were the only sentinels left to bear witness to the loss; we travelers only gawked and then drove on.

I hadn't yet learned how to fly fish still waters at that point in my life, so I would cast a worm into the deep water and wait for the bobber to be pulled under. It was possible to catch trout, but perch, walleye, bass, and catfish were just as likely to take the worm off your hook. I think one of the things my parents loved most about fishing the reservoir was that you could always catch something to take home.

Clarks Fork & Fool's Gold

On some trips, when distance from home rather than size of catch was the goal, we would travel up to Clarks Fork Canyon—a place that, later in life, would become one of my favorite locales. The environment at the mouth of the canyon closely reflected that of much of the Bighorn Basin. The Clarks Fork of the Yellowstone River drains the southeast corner of the Beartooth Mountains that span the Wyoming and Montana border and then, after exiting the canyon, carves its way through a semi-arid landscape. The waters of Clarks Fork produce a ribbon of blue and green in a landscape of browns and golds. Vegetation at the mouth of the canyon is sparse, as it is throughout the Bighorn Basin.

The uplands surrounding the Clarks Fork near the mouth of the canyon in many ways could not be more different from the tree-covered mountain uplands surrounding my mountain home-waters of Tensleep Creek. Trees here are sparse, even near the river. If you stand streamside and peer upslope, you'll see junipers that have slowly crept down the sides of the canyon to stake a tenuous claim as close as possible to the water's edge. Junipers have not quite made up their mind about which form they prefer along the Clarks Fork. You can find the aromatic evergreen as a tree, as well as spreading across the ground as a shrub, and with both forms in close proximity to each other. Both also provide, in large measure, the only year-round greenery to be found, although they are occasionally joined by limber pine.

While junipers have approached the river, the willows have claimed the edge of the water, taking root in sand- or silt-filled crevices between the rocks. A willow's site selection must be fortuitous in order for it to have any chance of surviving the river's yearlong current and the roaring spring runoff. I've often come to the Clarks Fork hoping for a chance to wet a fly prior to the initiation of spring runoff only to discover that I was too late and that the river was already thundering forth from the mouth of the canyon in a soil-laden torrent, carrying acres of loosened material downstream.

To complete the picture of a semi-arid oasis, prickly pear cactus and sharp-leaved yucca plants lurk just over the edge of the riverbanks, biding their time before they stab the unwary angler whose eyes are on the water rather than on the soft sandy soil. But cactus and yucca are not the only dangerous species lurking within this landscape: more than once I've had to negotiate my way to the water around an irritated rattlesnake.

Although fly fishing was my passion, the family trips to the Clarks Fork were also an opportunity to explore and to exercise my imagination. When walking along the edge of the water, hopping from rock to rock, a certain sparkle from a stone would sometimes catch my eye. Kneeling down, I would discover that there were flakes of gold trapped within them. If the desire to prospect for gold overcame my desire to fish, I would spend afternoons working with my stepbrothers, who had also noticed the sparkling stones, attempting to extract gold flakes from their rocky confines. Our favorite tactic consisted of using a sharp-edged rock about the size of a basketball to drop on either smaller rocks or the flat surface of large but thin stone panels that were oddly common. Hours upon hours were spent trying to extract the gold in this manner, although I don't think any of us ever succeeded in liberating even a single flake.

At some point, our parents finally let us in on a secret: the gold we were working so hard for was, in fact, iron pyrite or "fool's gold." After this revelation, it was common for one nonparticipating brother to approach our impromptu engineering site and inform us of our ignorance. But after some teasing and cajoling, the denouncer would be either run off or convinced that he was wrong and would be better employed by helping us make our fortunes "mining" the gold.

A SHORT HISTORY OF FISH STOCKING

It was during family fishing trips to the Clarks Fork that I first encountered Yellowstone cutthroat trout, the trout native to the mountains and valleys in which I had grown up. It would be years before I would have any appreciation of what it meant to catch a native trout of my home landscape, and it would be a few years beyond that before I would understand the ecological importance of discovering that native trout existed in only a fraction of their home range.

The idea that the trout I so loved to catch—be it rainbow, brown, or brook—were not a natural part of the landscape I loved would have been anathema to my perception of nature during this time. The concept of *native* had no meaning to me; the pleasure of exploring the world in pursuit of trout was what mattered. When I caught the black-spotted trout with the vivid orange slash under its jaw, I immediately recognized it was a different species, but I accorded it no more or less love than any other trout I caught. I also had no idea that many—in all likelihood, the vast majority—of the trout I caught were the product of fish hatcheries that churned out trout on an industrial scale. In fact, not far downstream from the mouth of the Clarks Fork Canyon, a fish hatchery resided alongside the river, just like the hatchery that sat at the foot of the Bighorn Mountains on the way to the cabin. My home-waters have been the recipient of a long and robust stocking program, and all the trout I caught on my home-waters beneath the cabin were likely raised in a hatchery.

Fish stocking has a distinguished—or, perhaps at this juncture, infamous—history throughout the United States and the world. Anders Halverson has traced the historical roots of fish propagation to 2100 B.C. China. Here in America, the eminent fish biologist Robert Behnke has traced the earliest fish propagation to Theodatus Garlick and his associate, Horace Ackley, beginning in 1853 near Cleveland, Ohio.[16] For the purposes of our discussion of trout stocking in the United States and particularly in the Rocky Mountains, the seminal moment in the advent of stocking trout and salmon outside of their native range is much closer to home. Livingston Stone's work on California's McCloud River beginning in 1872 is a critical chapter in the raising of trout for the purpose of stocking outside of their native range.[17] Stone's work on the

McCloud River produced profound impacts in the field of fish culture, while introducing the world to the McCloud River rainbow trout.

Why do we stock trout? The answer has shifted since the inception of the hatchery era in the United States. There were a number of reasons that the culturing of fish started to take place in America during the late nineteenth century: a decline in fish populations in waters heavily affected by industrial progress; a desire to see familiar fauna in new territories; social pressures (brook trout were looked upon as the gentlemen's pursuit of that day); and the impact of organizations known as acclimatization societies that actively sought to transport, raise, and establish non-native and exotic species in new locales throughout the world.

Halverson, in his study of the propagation and stocking of rainbow trout throughout the world, noted that "as a philosophy, acclimatization fit well with American ideas of progress and Manifest Destiny."[18] Thus fish stocking during the nineteenth and early twentieth centuries reflected the collective consciousness of the time, as it understood nature and its resources. Just as the forested wilderness was carved up by the axe and saw of progress and civilization, so were the waters encountered by an expanding American population manipulated to fit a preconceived notion of how nature should appear.

While public and private fish culturists sought to stock coldwaters to the brim with trout, they ran into the wall of ecological reality. While the pro-hatchery mood of the day assumed that nature often needed human "help" to make fisheries better,[19] in many waters, the huge numbers of trout produced diminishing returns. The reasons for these diminishing returns are varied, depending on the specific waters, but reflect the ecological constraints of habitat—whether it be the amount of food available, protection from predators, refugia from harsh seasonal conditions, or, critically for the establishment of a wild population, available spawning and rearing habitat. Ecological constraints such as these often result in the inability of stocked trout to establish a wild population, resulting in a perpetual cycle of stocking hatchery-raised trout.

The hatchery era, in addition to attempting to replenish diminished stocks resulting from environmental degradation, also stocked waters to support a seemingly insatiable demand for fishing. One means of addressing this appetite for trout was to stock full-grown fish ready to be caught by the angler, rather than stocking fry or fingerlings to feed and grow within the habitat to be caught as they matured. Thus was the "put-and-take" fishery established for catchable-sized trout. With the exception of the short period during which the fish are poured into a lake or stream and then pulled back out by a hook, their entire life is contained in hatchery facilities of one form or another.

Dam-building has produced countless reservoirs that have been the recipient of hatchery trout, oftentimes raised to be catchable-sized at the time of release. While dams create ideal habitat in the tailwaters below their outflows, the reservoirs formed from the impounded waters behind the dams are often seasonally too warm for native trout or destroy habitat, particularly spawning habitat. Such reservoirs have been perceived as an opportunity to stock catchable-sized trout that would not have been able to spawn following the loss of habitat after completion of the dam and the forming of the reservoir.

Trout Unlimited was established along the banks of the Au Sable River in Michigan in 1959, in part to end the madness associated with fishery policies based on stocking catchable trout in put-and-take fisheries. "A public fisheries program based on catchable trout is not natural resource management," exclaimed Robert Behnke in a 1991 article written for Trout Unlimited.[20] As evidenced by the birth of Trout Unlimited and its success in establishing wild trout fisheries, there has been a deep desire within the angling community to leave behind the hatchery era and the pursuit of trout raised in buildings and hatchery raceways. But there is another side to this coin. A large constituency had been created that not only supported hatcheries but expected catchable-sized trout to be dumped into their favorite waters for the sole purpose of being caught, often as quickly as possible, and taken home. The ability of this portion of the angling public to maintain pressure on the levers of state natural resource decision-making and funding is best demonstrated by the fact that twenty-five years after the widespread institution of catch-and-release fisheries, catchable-trout production had actually increased by 55 percent![21]

WYOMING HATCHERIES

My home state of Wyoming has a lengthy history of hatchery support and fish stocking, first as a territory and then later as a state. The practices were significant enough that a report on Wyoming's fishery management declared that "fishery management in Wyoming was born of fish culture." The same report noted that "most early agencies, including Wyoming, had the same mission; spawn, hatch, and rear trout."[22] This long history of stocking has continued through to today, although hatcheries within Wyoming, as with so many other states, have partially transitioned to a new mission, that of conservation.

A number of hatcheries now reserve portions of their facilities for producing native trout. Natives cultured and reared in these facilities can be used to bolster and, in many cases, restore native species to their historical habitat following removal of non-natives that were intentionally stocked in years past. Taken a step further, hatcheries can house genetically pure broodstock for replenishing genetically depleted populations or serve as a temporary housing facility for a unique or threatened population while their native range is purged of invaders.[23]

Like the then territory of Wyoming from which it was carved, Yellowstone—the United States' first national park—was unable to escape the stocking of its pristine waters. An early park superintendent, Captain Frazier Boutelle, complained about the scarcity of fish:

> In passing through the Park I noticed with surprise the barrenness of most of the water in the Park. Besides the beautiful Shoshone and other small lakes there are hundreds of miles of as fine streams as any in existence without a fish of any kind. . . . I hope . . . to see all of these waters so stocked that the pleasure-seeker in the Park can enjoy fine fishing within a few rods of any hotel or camp.[24]

Captain Boutelle's thoughts on fish stocking were penned in 1891 during the era in which the U.S. Army oversaw and managed the park and its resources. The hatchery craze of the day gripped Yellowstone National Park and its administrators early, and a hatchery was established on the banks of Yellowstone

Lake around the year 1900. By 1980, more than 310 million native and non-native trout had been stocked throughout Yellowstone.[25] As much as 40 percent of the park's waters that were stocked had been barren of fish at the time of Yellowstone's establishment.[26] Species that were stocked included native and non-native trout, Atlantic and Coho salmon, and black bass,[27] and—not to be overlooked—the lake trout that would eventually be illegally stocked in Yellowstone Lake, decimating the cutthrout trout population (more on this in chapter 13). Lewis Lake is believed to be the most likely source for the lake trout illegally introduced into Yellowstone Lake.[28] Historically fishless, Lewis Lake is believed to have received 17,903 lake trout between the years of 1890 and 1941, in addition to brown trout, cutthroat trout, and grayling.[29]

The Lake Fish Hatchery would eventually produce 818 million trout eggs, which were primarily stocked in waters outside of Yellowstone over the hatchery's fifty-seven-year life span.[30] Today, Yellowstone's fishery management policy emphasizes preservation of the park's native species and their habitat. Non-natives are quite likely to continue occupying many of Yellowstone's waters, at least in the foreseeable future, but native fish are supported through a multitude of policies. One particular policy of interest for the angling community is liberalized harvest numbers for non-natives on many waters within the park, while catch-and-release is the policy for native fish.[31] This policy has resulted in an angling opportunity not to be missed, both for its unparalleled angling experience, as well as the opportunity to catch trout in support of conservation.

From the early days of fish culture through today, one of the main, if not central, purposes of hatcheries was to raise trout for the express purpose of stocking them for recreation and consumption by the angler. As time has passed and science has begun to provide the data necessary to demonstrate the negative effects of stocking non-natives outside of their home range, our ecological understanding of the importance of maintaining ecosystems and their native species has increased. This understanding, coupled with increased environmental awareness and willingness to act, as evidenced through national legislation such as the Endangered Species Act, has allowed the role of hatcheries to evolve. A number of hatcheries now operate with the explicit purpose of culturing and raising species that are either listed as "threatened" or "endangered" under the Endangered Species Act.

Although aquaculture, in certain circumstances, has helped to stabilize a flagging native population or restore a lost population, hatcheries are not a panacea. This is not to say that in the contemporary era, hatcheries do not a have a role to play in maintaining native trout species and populations, but we need to be cognizant of the limitations, from both an ecological and an economic standpoint. Hatcheries throughout the nation continue to raise and churn out non-natives for stocking in waters outside their native range. In Wyoming the ten hatcheries and rearing stations produce natives and non-natives alike. The Wyoming Game and Fish Department has even produced unnatural strains of trout. Two examples are the splake, which is a cross between a brook trout and a lake trout, and the tiger trout, which is a cross between a brook trout and a brown trout. Both of these hatchery-created species are purported to be infertile, and Robert Behnke notes that there is no known natural hybridization between brook trout and lake trout within the native range of the two species, although tiger trout do rarely occur in nature.[32] Of course, the brown trout is a native of Europe, and therefore brook trout and brown trout would never encounter each other, unless in a hatchery or in waters where one or both have been stocked outside their native range. Nevertheless, the novelty of the two hatchery-created species has produced a sport constituency for these human-concocted hybrid fish that supports continued production of both, which, in turn, creates yet another impediment to restoring native populations.

CHAPTER 7

The Wilderness Trout Paradox

WITH THE GENTLEST OF CALLS, the cabin, and the waters that flowed past, whispered to me through the years of my absence during high school and college. I finally heeded the call the summer after I graduated from the University of Wyoming, when I returned to the cabin for only the third time since my grandmother had passed away. I learned one of the most valuable lessons that home-waters had to teach during those tumultuous college years, as I lived each day without much care of what came next, reveling in the uncertainty of the future, guided only by the coarsest contours of life.

By this time in my life, I had been a soldier in the Army National Guard for more than four years. On September 11, 2001, my roommate had woken me up, his face pale, and said, "We're under attack." I couldn't figure out what the hell he meant until he pulled me to the TV to watch the horror unfold. I watched the stomach-churning footage of people flinging themselves from windows in the World Trade Center towers, with the realization that I would be going to war. A year and a half later in March 2003, I watched the opening of the war in Iraq from a hotel room in Rawlins, Wyoming. I had been traveling from my National Guard drill to meet some friends in Las Vegas for spring break, but a blizzard closed every road around me and I never made it there. Although war preparations commenced in 2003, the call didn't come for me while I was still attending college. I loved being a soldier more than anything else except perhaps fly fishing, so after graduating, I went down to the army recruiting office and reenlisted, this time into the active duty branch of the army, leaving the National Guard and Wyoming behind.

The summer between graduation and my date to leave for active duty was filled with excitement, heartbreak, and trepidation. I had only the vaguest sense of what was in store for me but that was part of the thrill, one enhanced by the transition from college—and its carefree, live-in-the-moment spontaneity—to an uncertain but exciting career in an army at war. It was in this most uncertain of moments in my life that the gentle whisper from Rubyat reached me. But this time, there was something else, a secret behind the whisper—and a teasing meaning: the hidden truth that in order to return home, you first have to leave. With this idea in my mind, I made the decision to explore beyond Rubyat and venture into the wild mountains and valleys deeper in the Bighorn Mountains. I would head to the area that held the snowpack that, after melting and flowing down bare granite slope, eventually became Tensleep Creek.

The Cloud Peak Wilderness

If you look upstream from the waters below the cabin, you can see the mountains of the Cloud Peak Wilderness looming on the horizon above the tops of pine trees. I began my ascent on the trail that led into the wilderness dressed in a short-sleeved shirt, shorts, and a baseball cap, with my pack on my back and my old yellow-and-brown fly rod strapped to the top. Growing up, I had heard stories from my grandfather, uncles, and even my dad about their adventures fishing the waters of the Cloud Peak, and particularly Lake Solitude, and I had decided that this high-altitude lake would be the destination for my first solo backcountry trip.

The map in my backpack showed me the general contours of the mountains and valleys I would ascend and cross during the course of my journey. It also had a line that supposedly depicted the trail I was following, but like so much of life, the contours on the map only hinted at what the world offers when you choose to explore it. I carefully sidestepped the horse-apples in the trail as I bent over at the waist, shrugged my shoulders to adjust my pack, and continued my ascent. Sharing a Wyoming wilderness trail with backcountry horsemen is part of the character of the trail I cherish. After emerging from the dense forest trail and cresting a small hill, I found myself at the first in a series of lakes that I would pass on my way to Lake Solitude. The sight of the waters of Lake Helen nearly stopped my heart with its alpine beauty! This is why I had come to the wilderness: to cast flies to trout that only a select few would ever seek out.

Lake Helen, Lake Marion, Misty Moon: I would pass each on my way to Lake Solitude. On a later trip, I would spend several days base-camped at Lake Marion, as I sought to catch trout in every body of water within a half-day's journey from camp. Family lore holds that Lake Marion is named after my great-grandmother Marion Johnson. According to this story, my great-grandmother—known to me as Grandma Mimi—and her father, Ruby, had taken a trip on horseback into the wilderness; this was long before the area was known as the Cloud Peak Wilderness. While on their excursion, they encountered the local Forest Service ranger near an unnamed lake. Ruby and my great-grandmother, then only a young girl, struck up a conversation with the ranger as all sat astride horses. At one point during the conversation, the ranger turned to my great-grandmother and asked her if she would like to have a lake named after her. Of course, agreed my Grandma Mimi; what young lady wouldn't be thrilled by such a proposition? The ranger pointed at the lake ahead of them and told her that it would carry her name, and once he got off the mountain, he would be sure to make it official.

It was during my trip the summer after college that I learned the difference between a perceived wilderness and true *wildness*. When traveling mountain roads to the cabin, there were Forest Service campgrounds, as well as roadside lakes, rivers, and streams; all were screened in seclusion by thick forests, giving one a feeling of rugged western wilderness. These trips had left me with the feeling that I knew the Wyoming wilderness, but there was an aspect of wildness that I never knew I was missing: solitude. As I stepped onto the trail with my pack on my shoulders from the trailhead at West Tensleep Lake, and as I advanced beyond the first quarter mile from a trailhead into designated wilderness, I was introduced to true western *wildness*. The farther each step carried me from the trailhead, the vaster I found the world around me, as I weaved in and out of the forest, ascending the mountain trail. In the first few steps, I left behind the site of the campground and trailhead parking lot. A few more strides and the sounds of vehicle engines and voices from the picnic area were swallowed by the forest. After crossing the stream, and for the remainder of the trip, encounters with other human beings would be the exception rather than the norm. I quickly learned that true wilderness is best experienced in lonesome solitude.

SEARCHING FOR GOLDEN TROUT

When you are standing on the edge of an alpine lake surrounded by towering gray granite formations reflected in the water's mirrored surface, casting to trout seems the logical extension of this wilderness portrait. But wilderness and trout are a bit of a paradox. Fishing for and catching trout in unblemished mountain waters flanked by jagged spires is the pinnacle of fly fishing heaven for many. I have sipped from this cup a number of times and always returned for more. But very often, particularly in the Rocky Mountains, the trout we pursue and catch are much like the trout we find at lower elevations and outside wilderness areas: stocked fish from hatcheries or wild populations of previously stocked non-native trout.

During a trip in which I was base-camped at Lake Marion with a buddy from high school, we fished every body of water with gusto, but it was a very specific species of trout we were intent on pursuing—golden trout. This species of trout incorporates the traits that many anglers desire most in their quarry. Although diminutive when compared to other trout, golden trout are notoriously finicky when it comes to taking a fly, and they make up in color what they lack in size. The ability to trick a trout, especially a wary trout, into striking a fly is considered the height of the fly fishing art, and golden trout sit perched atop the highest rung of the finicky ladder. Golden trout also require exceptionally cold, clear, and clean high-mountain waters to survive, so anglers are drawn to remote and hidden wilderness lakes and streams to pursue these delicate wonders.

The golden trout that Terry and I pursued with unanswered patience are not native to the waters of the Cloud Peak Wilderness, the Bighorn Mountains, or the state of Wyoming; this vibrant little trout, whose beauty is reflected in the remote mountain wilderness in which they've been stocked, are native to the Sierra Nevada. The waters of the Cloud Peak Wilderness were probably barren of fish when Euro-American exploration and settlement of the valleys below was under way in the mid-to-late 1800s. Yellowstone cutthroat trout swam in the lower waters, but a series of falls likely prevented migration of the trout to the highest mountain waters. The disconnected alpine lakes and ponds were even more likely than headwater streams to have been fishless prior to being stocked in the Johnny Appleseed–like plantings that followed the birth of the hatchery era. The early hatchery era saw tiny trout transported to remote waters via horses and milk cans, among other innovative methods.

It has been estimated that as many as sixteen thousand high-mountain lakes in the western United States were fishless when the descendants of Europeans first laid eyes upon them.[33] Like lower elevation waters, these fishless ponds and headwater streams, not to mention the occasional large mountain lake, were stocked with fish from across the United States and, in some instances, from across the Atlantic Ocean. The stocking of fishless waters for sport recreation was undertaken with zeal during the hatchery era, and high-altitude waters like those found in what would become the Cloud Peak Wilderness were no exception. However, the continued stocking of waters in wilderness does not sit well with many, as the activity runs counter to the definition of wilderness established in the Wilderness Act of 1964, which envisions modern wilderness as "untrammeled by man, where man himself is a visitor and does not remain."

WHAT IS WILDERNESS?

Wilderness in the modern world is a strange thing. In the lower forty-eight states, it is no longer the dark primeval forests that challenged frontiersmen and stymied the expansion of society across the landscape. Today, wilderness no longer consists of boundless tracks of forest to be subjugated by axe and

saw—that was accomplished long ago. No, *wilderness* today is a legal definition and a boundary drawn on a map, made possible only by the restraint im-
posed by the Wilderness Act. Activists and politicians with a sense of foresight
recognized the need to protect those portions of America's landscape that had
escaped timber harvest and the road building that accompanied industrial-
level forestry, which had pushed development deeper and deeper into virgin
landscapes. They recognized that protections would be needed to ensure that
some undeveloped areas remained: thus, the Wilderness Act was born.

Wilderness designation sets aside portions of ecosystems that are less disturbed by the hand of man. Nevertheless, there is often a misconception that
wilderness is pristine and reflects what the land looked like when Meriwether
Lewis and William Clark first traveled west (it is worth noting that Lewis
and Clark didn't travel through the Bighorn Mountains during their Corps of
Discovery explorations that lasted from May 1804 through September 1806).
In the lower forty-eight states, it is much more likely that the evidence of man
and his impacts to the landscape have simply been reduced within areas of
designated wilderness. Within these areas, there may not be signs of mining
and timber cutting, but evidence of man comes in the form of bridges built
over streams along trails maintained for recreation or in the ubiquitous grazing of free-range cattle.

For some, the stocking of wilderness waters with trout that did not evolve
in that landscape diminishes the wildness of the wilderness they've sought out.
The artificial nature of stocking, and especially the stocking of non-native
fish, conflicts with the idea that in a wilderness area, the mark of man should
not be left upon the land. For these people, it matters little whether the fish
stocked into wilderness waters arrived via milk can on a horse or were dumped
from the belly of a helicopter; the wild character of the lands set aside as wilderness has been tarnished.

Recreational angling is the locus of fish stocking in wilderness and non-
wilderness waters alike. The continued stocking of trout into wilderness waters today is likely the result not of recreational pressure from the harvest of
fish but of the lack of food and habitat to support a self-sustaining population, particularly in alpine lakes and ponds that offer little to no spawning

habitat. Herein we find an additional facet of the wilderness trout paradox: in order for people to continue to fish for trout in wilderness waters, the wild character of the land must itself be compromised. This elevation of angling above other wilderness values is what has driven at least a portion of the resistance to the stocking of wilderness waters. But beyond even that, there are the ecological impacts to wilderness waters from stocking historically fishless waters.

Golden trout may very well be the epitome of wilderness trout, but in the Cloud Peak, they are as exotic as the brook trout I always seem to catch, even when chasing golden trout. Whenever a trout, any trout, is stocked into a historically fishless water, it immediately becomes an exotic species. Disruptions to the delicate alpine food web are immediate and long term, since the introduced trout is likely to become the water's apex predator. Impacts can ripple from the water itself to the terrestrial environment, as reptile and amphibian populations are decimated.[34] The recognition of the ecological impacts of stocking trout into fishless wilderness waters, and the lack of a scientific basis for such ecological tinkering, underpins yet another aspect of the resistance to the stocking of trout into wilderness waters.[35]

A LAST REFUGE & A LARGER PROBLEM

The final aspect of the wilderness trout paradox that needs to be considered is that wilderness waters can serve as a refuge for many native species in peril today. Populations of healthy and uncompromised natives, such as the greenback cutthroat trout of Colorado, are tucked away in difficult-to-reach alpine lakes and headwater streams protected by downstream barriers. It is an ecological paradox that the stocking of natives into originally fishless waters within their native range and in waters outside their range has preserved some pure populations of native species—and in some cases, the only remaining population of a species. That is to say, in some cases, an entire species or unique population can be found only in these refuges. Robert Behnke relates just such a tale in the conservation of greenback cutthroat trout in his magnum opus *Trout and Salmon of North America*.[36]

We must recognize that there is an ecological consequence whenever we choose to stock imperiled native species into either fishless or wilderness waters. The impacts of such an action must be weighed accordingly—an aspect of fish stocking that has often been ignored when stocking wilderness waters.[37] The remoteness of many of the waters found in wilderness areas has, in some cases, allowed species threatened with local extirpation or extinction to maintain a tenuous grip on their existence. Even for species like the Yellowstone cutthroat trout, which is not currently in danger of extinction, wilderness waters serve as a bastion for the continuation of the species free from competition and hybridization with other species of trout. The stocking of wilderness waters must be considered as part of the conservation solution, so long as natives continue to lose habitat, populations are threatened with extinction, and important genes are in danger of being lost to the species forever.

While wilderness waters serve as a temporary reprieve for threatened native species as they continue to lose ground at lower elevations, wilderness waters are only a partial solution. In many cases, the waters in which native species reside are either high-mountain lakes disconnected from any other waters or headwaters streams protected from downstream threats by a physical barrier to movement. This ultimately creates a conservation challenge when it comes to reversing the trend of shrinking ranges of native species.

A key component to ensuring the long-term health of a species, whether terrestrial or aquatic, is the interconnection of populations across the landscape. Individual populations of a species that have the freedom to travel throughout their home range allows for the strengthening of the species through the passing of genetic material between populations. Interconnectedness also provides species survival insurance. When a population has become locally extinct, the territory it once inhabited becomes available for others of the species to colonize and reproduce within, assuming that the now vacant territory is still suitable for habitation. The disconnected nature of many, if not most, wilderness waters prevents the interconnection necessary for long-term survival of threatened native trout populations. So while this disconnectedness protects the species, it also hinders their long-term conservation expansion back into their native waters.

The disconnected nature of wilderness trout populations is a symptom of a larger problem of habitat fragmentation throughout the Rocky Mountains. In some cases, the fragmentation is part of an attempt to protect remaining native populations; in other cases, it is the outcome of poorly planned natural resource management. Rivers, streams, and tributaries throughout these mountains have become disconnected by dams and the reservoirs behind them, by road culverts, and by the, at times, intentional man-made barriers aimed at preventing the movement of natives and non-natives alike. The ultimate outcome is a fragmented landscape with populations of native species that are physically disassociated from one another, even if they inhabit the same watershed.

Wilderness trout—for that is what many native populations, if not entire species, have become—are important for conservation, as well as for angling. We are blessed to have, within our wilderness areas, the opportunity to chase both native and non-native trout in some of the most beautiful landscapes in the lower forty-eight states. The opportunity to cast a fly to a trout in absolute solitude beneath the uninterrupted grandeur of mountain peaks is a remarkable experience, one of sublime delicacy. Casting a small caddis fly in a high-mountain wilderness pond to a brook trout that hasn't consumed anything other than midges all season long does nothing to diminish the sublime quality of the experience for me, although I know it does for some. For me, the experience is enhanced by my knowledge that the high-spirited little brook trout is not a native to that pond, which allows me to appreciate what that means in the context of the broader environment. My experience is deepened, however, when the opportunity arises to cast to a native whose lineage is protected within wilderness waters, rare as those opportunities may be.

Wilderness fly fishing experiences should not be dismissed just because many of the once fishless waters are now home to non-native trout. Wilderness is grander than this, and its waters are capable of providing both sport and sanctuary. Our knowledge of the trout we catch in wilderness waters and what it means for the larger conservation picture is a vital component of the wilderness experience, one that should enhance that experience, not detract from it. These opportunities provide us with both knowledge and a personal sense of the future gains that are possible when combining the sport of fly fishing with native trout conservation.

Now that I'm aware of the impacts associated with the stocking of non-native fish outside their ranges, as well as the stocking of fish into once fishless waters, will I forgo chasing golden trout in the Cloud Peak Wilderness? Well, no. I still look forward to catching the elusive quarry in such a beautiful landscape, but I also would not object if the Wyoming Game and Fish Department decides to no longer stock the waters of the Cloud Peak with the Sierra Nevada native. I will also continue to push for the reintroduction of extirpated natives to their home-waters. While this may appear somewhat hypocritical, I prefer to think of it as pragmatism. There are numerous problems plaguing our aquatic ecosystems, some of which may be reversed, others that may be mitigated, and still others that cannot be solved with today's technology and innovation—and some that may never be solved. I will continue to support solutions to both building and restoring native trout and wilderness watersheds, but as these solutions develop and are implemented, I will also continue to be an angler who is able to cherish what he finds on the landscape, even while recognizing that there is a chance that the best is still yet to come.

CHAPTER 8

Going Native

WHEN OUR COMBAT TOUR WAS complete, my unit returned to Baumholder, Germany, where we were put on thirty days of mandatory leave. Within days of returning from that leave, we were assembled as a battalion and informed that we would be returning to Iraq in just under a year: we had just received our warning order to again prepare for combat. Preparing to return to Iraq meant longer days than what was typical, even in the army, and I often spent what little downtime we had in the quiet and cramped confines of my barracks room.

One night, while watching the Armed Forces Network (or AFN, as the channel reminded us ad nauseam during pseudo-commercial interruptions on the tiny TV/VCR combo in my barracks room), I happened onto a show about Yellowstone National Park. AFN provides popular American television programs to overseas services members, and on this particular evening, I was fortunate enough to catch the rebroadcast of a PBS program. As I watched high-altitude camera shots roll over the mountains and valleys of Yellowstone, the pull to return to Rubyat and my home-waters again swept over me. The show also left me with a newly awakened interest in environmental issues, which sent me back to the PX to pick up a copy of a book I had noticed earlier: Jared Diamond's *Collapse: How Societies Choose to Fail or Succeed*. As I read the book, quickly devouring it at night, I began to internalize its message about society's dependence on natural resources and the consequences of shortsighted environmental destructiveness. From within my tiny brick and concrete barracks room, a burgeoning sense of the larger world around me was awakened.

As it happened, I did not end up returning to Iraq with the 4/27th Field Artillery Battalion. Instead, and much to my astonishment, the army decided to send me stateside to pursue a master's degree and a commission as an officer. And so, not long after my environmental awakening in my barracks room in Germany, I found myself—with more than a little guilt—on my way to graduate school.

A VIEW FROM NEW ENGLAND

I soon found myself in unfamiliar territory: New England. I began attending graduate school at the University of New Hampshire in Durham within days of returning stateside. As a student in the political science department, I quickly began to nurture the seed that had been planted in my barracks room, and I threw myself into the study of environmental politics and policy. I chose for my thesis research topic something that would engage my passion and give me an excuse to return to the Rocky Mountains: the trout native to my home-waters, the Yellowstone cutthroat trout. At the time, the Yellowstone cutthroat trout had been petitioned for listing under the Endangered Species Act and, like so many species petitioned for listing, the decision was being challenged in the courts.

It was at this point that I made my first connection with the science of ecology that deepened my love of nature. No longer was I satisfied with simply viewing nature and appreciating its art, subtlety, and grandeur. Through the study of ecology, my eyes were opened to understanding why the patterns in nature I saw existed in the configuration in which I found them. The connections between species through predation, competition, and the myriad other interactions that shaped nature began to reveal themselves. I have found few events in life as empowering as studying ecology. Now when I approach the stream, I appreciate the beauty of what I find there through a heightened awareness that helps me understand, at least in the broadest of senses, the incredible complexity of the natural world. The vast complexity of nature enhances the visual, auditory, and olfactory beauty that comprises a trout stream. Even though, at best, we are likely to view only the most mundane threads of nature's tapestry, it is still nearly enough to dwarf human comprehension.

The waters of New England differed from the familiar mountain streams of the Rockies, as much as the deciduous forests differed from the lodgepole pines I knew so well. Many of the rivers I passed every day were tidal, and they waxed and waned with the pull of the moon. This is not to say that the waters lacked trout, as I would learn from the wonderful folks I would meet at the local Trout Unlimited meetings, who took a displaced Wyoming kid and accepted him as one of their own.

While studying environmental policy and ecology at the University of New Hampshire, I was introduced to urban fisheries and coastal waters. Through Trout Unlimited and the friends I found there, I also learned of the local love for the region's native trout—the brook trout. Although the spunky little trout had been ubiquitous throughout the mountain streams I had grown up fishing in Wyoming, I quickly learned how much ground it had lost in its native range in New England as a result of the Industrial Revolution and the subsequent urbanization. The passion for trout conservation I discovered in the Great Bay chapter of Trout Unlimited deepened my love and longing for my own distant home-waters.

The intertwined passion for trout and fly fishing was evident at every Trout Unlimited meeting I attended. But the deepest and most foundational of all passions could be boiled down to a single unifying theme—the love of catching a native. I learned that in New England, the passion for catching natives included not only trout but also salmon. The love of brook trout was nearly unanimous, as much as I could tell (although the love of sport, trout, and conservation, in general, was never in question either). Beyond love of the native brook trout, there were those whose passion was the elusive "salter": sea-run brook trout that, if the stories I heard were even partially true, had once been abundant and widespread but today were so rare as to be almost mythological. There was a small group of anglers I got to know who enjoyed catching trout on a fly but who truly lived for the chance to cast to running

Atlantic salmon. For them, the year was delineated more by the life cycle of the Atlantic salmon than by the seasons.

The New England passion I found for fly fishing and conservation inspired me to carry that passion home, which I was able to do when I traveled back to the Rocky Mountains to conduct research for my thesis in the summer of 2006. Crashing on a friend's couch for weeks at a time, I traveled throughout the Greater Yellowstone Ecosystem, learning all I could from fishery managers, public land managers, and nonprofit conservation organizations, which included Trout Unlimited. My project deepened my understanding of fishery policy and ecology, but perhaps more importantly, it allowed me to reconnect with my home-waters for the first time after coming home from war.

THE MISSING YELLOWSTONE CUTTHROAT TROUT

I returned home to study the trout native to my home landscape, but the native was no longer to be found in my home-waters. Yellowstone cutthroat trout had long ago succumbed to the ecological pressures of having non-native trout stocked into their habitat, and—just as when I was a child—brook, brown, and rainbow trout inhabited the stream below the cabin. My early understanding of ecology was shaped by the fauna I discovered in the stream after my dry fly disappeared from the surface of the water. Until I went to graduate school, I had assumed that the trout I pulled from the waters below the cabin were as much a part of the native fauna as the deer, elk, and eagles that inhabited the Wyoming landscape.

Having to confront my lack of ecological knowledge was initially difficult for me, since it forced me to recognize that the trout I had loved so much were not native to the waters I also loved. This recognition also raised an important question for me: What exactly does it mean to be native? The answer, I learned, from both my research on Yellowstone cutthroat trout for my thesis and my coursework in ecology, is that, in ecological terms, to be native is to have evolved in the landscape in which a species is found. The brook, brown, and rainbow trout I found waiting for me in my home-waters were no more native than were the carp from Asia found in the warmer waters in the basins below the mountains or the ring-necked pheasants, also imported from Asia, that are so sought after by upland game hunters.

Learning that the trout I loved would have been unknown in the waters that the earliest generation of my family encountered as they settled in Wyoming generated a fair amount of cognitive dissonance for me—which only deepened as I delved further into the study of ecology. I learned that the rainbow trout is native to the west coast of the United States, while the brook trout is native to the Great Lakes region, much of New England, and the Appalachian Mountains (as well as great expanses of Canada). I learned that the wily brown trout—the species I tended to catch least in Tensleep Creek but the one that tended to be the largest of the three species of trout I caught each summer—was a native of Europe. As I learned more about these three species of trout, I had to come to grips with what the term *non-native* meant ecologically, as well as how the term informed environmental policy. The term struck a strange chord with me, since these non-native species were so closely linked in my mind with the serene environs I had known for so many years.

The Yellowstone cutthroat trout native to my home landscape is one of fourteen subspecies of cutthroat trout, all of which are native only to western North America. With the exception of lake trout, cutthroat trout are the most widely distributed species of trout in North America.[38] The Yellowstone cutthroat trout (YCT for short) is found in the Upper Snake River above the Shoshone Falls in Idaho, as well as in the Yellowstone River watershed from which it takes its name, so its range occupies both sides of the Continental Divide. On the east side of the Continental Divide, its range extends down the east side of the Rocky Mountains, across the Bighorn Basin, and up the Tongue River, whose headwaters reside within the Bighorn Mountains.[39] The unusual circumstance that allowed the species to occupy both sides of the

Rocky Mountains is the result of the Continental Divide straddling Two Ocean Creek in the Bridger-Teton National Forest, located generally south of Yellowstone National Park. Two Ocean Creek possesses one branch that drains to the Gulf of Mexico and a second branch that drains to the Pacific Ocean;[40] the two branches are aptly named Atlantic Creek and Pacific Creek. It continues to be possible for Yellowstone cutthroat trout to cross the Continental Divide to this day, since there are no barriers to movement between the two branches of the stream.[41] Writing in their insightful volume *Yellowstone Fishes: Ecology, History, and Angling in the Park*, John Varley and Paul Schullery note that both the upper Yellowstone River and Yellowstone Lake were barren of fish until some intrepid individuals of the namesake subspecies crossed the Continental Divide over Two Ocean Pass.[42]

The most striking feature of the Yellowstone cutthroat trout (or any cutthroat trout) is the namesake red or orange slash that runs beneath the jaw. The fish is a striking golden yellow, with rich tones that deepen from its belly, moving up the flanks and toward the back. Black spots are present from the dorsal fin to the belly of the trout, with the majority of these large spots concentrated on and near the tail.

A second subspecies, recognized by its small spotted markings, occupies some of the same watersheds in the Snake River as the YCT. Found only in the Snake River portion of the Yellowstone cutthroat trout's native range, the Snake River finespotted cutthroat trout is covered in profuse small spots. Robert Behnke has described this subspecies as having the smallest spots of any cutthroat trout, likening them to flecks of ground pepper.[43] Once considered a variation of the Yellowstone cutthroat trout, it is now recognized as a subspecies unto itself, after having been described in Behnke's 1992 work on western trout; it has since been bestowed the befitting scientific name of *Oncorhynchus clarki behnkei*.[44] While the Snake River finespotted cutthroat trout has been identified taxonomically as a separate subspecies, both it and the Yellowstone cutthroat trout are often treated as the same subspecies for the purpose of management although not necessarily for the purpose of conservation. A range-wide status assessment prepared for the Yellowstone cutthroat trout, partially in response to the petitioning of the trout under the

Endangered Species Act, recognizes two forms of YCT rather than two separate subspecies, choosing to punt on the question by noting that although there are clearly visible characteristics that separate the two, there is currently no way to differentiate the subspecies based on genetic analysis related to spotting patterns.[45] Nevertheless, management agencies recognize the clear need to protect diversity at both the species and population levels. Thus, in Wyoming, the two different forms of Yellowstone cutthroat trout are not stocked over the top of each other.[46]

Although I became familiar with Yellowstone cutthroat trout by catching them in the North Fork of the Shoshone River and the Clarks Fork of the Yellowstone, they are not simply river or stream trout. The YCT has a number of different life histories, including those of Yellowstone Lake fame, which historically grew to tremendous size, though not as large as the Lahontan cutthroat trout of Pyramid Lake in Nevada! Researchers have recognized that many unique life histories have already been lost among western trout within their native ranges, which adds an additional confounding factor to the task of preserving native trout. As noted in the range-wide assessment for the Yellowstone cutthroat trout, those populations least affected and most genetically pure are most likely to reside in headwater streams where they are disconnected from other populations of YCT and from the non-natives that would otherwise outcompete, prey upon, and hybridize with them.[47] Such fragmentation reduces the overall health of the Yellowstone cutthroat trout subspecies by preventing gene flow between populations and by preventing recolonization of areas, in the event that a population is lost to, say, a surge of toxic waters from a mine site or a mudflow following a catastrophic wildfire. In addition to the ripple effects such losses have throughout ecosystems and food webs, these losses of unique life histories steal from us and from our children the opportunity to encounter species in their original, native habitats.

Of the fourteen subspecies of cutthroat trout, two are extinct: the yellowfin cutthroat trout of Twin Lakes, Colorado, and the Alvord cutthroat trout of the Alvord Basin in Oregon and Nevada. The greenback cutthroat trout, originally native to the Front Range of Colorado, including the Arkansas and South Platte drainages above five thousand feet,[48] was believed to have gone extinct, as well, prior to the 1953 discovery of a remnant population in a small stream within the South Platte watershed.[49] A robust recovery program was undertaken to bring the greenback cutthroat trout back from the brink of extinction, which resulted in the subspecies being reclassified from "endangered" to "threatened" in 1978.[50] A curveball was thrown at the recovery program in 2012, when the results from a genetic study revealed that the fish being raised and stocked as greenback cutthroat trout were likely genetically compromised as a result of liberal historical stocking practices. The research identified Bear Creek along the Front Range as containing what is likely the sole remaining pure population of greenback cutthroat trout.[51]

The greenback is joined by the Lahontan cutthroat and the Paiute cutthroat trout in receiving protections under the Endangered Species Act. When I began working on this book, the Rio Grande cutthroat trout was a candidate for listing under the Endangered Species Act, but in October of 2014, the U.S. Fish and Wildlife Service made the determination that the subspecies was not imperiled to the extent that it required the protections offered under the Endangered Species Act.[52]

The U.S. Fish and Wildlife Service has been petitioned at various times to consider four other subspecies of cutthroat for listing under the Endangered Species Act, including the Yellowstone cutthroat trout. Although the service has declined to list all but the three subspecies mentioned above, the trend for cutthroat trout is not exactly encouraging. The Yellowstone cutthroat trout was originally petitioned for listing under the Endangered Species Act in 1998. A required ninety-day review of the petition was not completed until 2001. The Fish and Wildlife Service was then sued in 2004, which resulted in a twelve-month status assessment that, like the 2001 review, determined that the subspecies did not warrant being listed as either threatened or endangered, since the subspecies was considered to still be widely distributed throughout its native range.[53] But there is more to this story than there may seem.

The second iteration of a range-wide state assessment of the Yellowstone cutthroat trout was completed in 2006 (the first was completed in 2001), to help determine the extent to which the subspecies was imperiled.[54] The assessment found that Yellowstone cutthroat trout could be found in only 43 percent of their historical habitat and that many of those populations were in disconnected headwaters. Even though Yellowstone cutthroat trout were found to still reside in 43 percent of their historical habitat, only 28 percent of remaining populations were free from the influences of hybridization with other trout. What this means is that not only are many of the remaining populations of Yellowstone cutthroat trout in disconnected habitat unable to recolonize much of their lost habitat but that nearly three quarters of the remaining populations are further at risk due to the stocking of non-natives into the waters in which Yellowstone cutthroat trout remain. Why does this matter? Because this gives us an idea of how fragile the overall Yellowstone cutthroat trout population truly is—and this is one of the subspecies that is *not* currently threatened with the possibility of extinction by the standards of those who are the gatekeepers of the Endangered Species Act.

In a 1981 essay on the Paiute cutthroat trout, Behnke called the hatchery-focused era of fishery management the "dark ages of fisheries management." He noted that the stocking of non-native trout into the habitat of natives during this era resulted in "the virtual extinction of the native cutthroat trout throughout vast areas—such as the entire Lahontan Basin."[55] There are numerous reasons why the Yellowstone cutthroat trout that are native to my home-waters have declined so dramatically. Habitat loss and degradation as a result of human activities along with angler harvest all play a role in the overall decline of the YCT, but it is the stocking of non-native trout into the YCT's native range that exacerbates the situation and is likely the largest threat to the subspecies and its individual populations.[56] And it is here that the angling community, as conservation gatekeepers, can have a profound impact on the future of native trout by voicing their support and putting their money to work for the conservation, restoration, and protection of native trout and the cessation of stocking in waters that can continue to serve as viable habitat for native trout.

A WIDER DECLINE

Livestock grazing, logging, mining, and irrigation: these are the Four Horsemen of the Apocalypse for trout, according to Thomas McGuane in his introduction to Behnke's *Trout and Salmon of North America*. Missing from this multitude of resource-extractive industries is the ecological pollution of non-native stocking. Perhaps the salmon-conservation-oriented acronym "4-H," which stands for hatcheries, harvest, hydropower, and habitat, is even more appropriate for our discussion. In all likelihood, the chances of survival for native trout will continue to be driven downward by a dark combination of all these factors.

The fate of the Yellowstone cutthroat trout of my home-waters only scratches the surface of native trout species in decline. In addition to the cutthroat trout subspecies noted above, the bull trout is listed as threatened throughout its remaining range, as is the Gila trout of the Gila River Basin of New Mexico and the Apache trout of the Salt River Basin of Arizona. Add to this list the golden trout of the Little Kern River of the Sierra Nevada, and you begin to get the picture; and we've only discussed trout, omitting the numerous salmon populations that have been declared threatened or endangered, and we haven't even broached the subject of native non-sport fishes that are critical components of their aquatic ecosystems but are easily overlooked by all but the most conscientious of anglers and studious fisheries biologists.

In the last one hundred or so years, native trout have faltered under the onslaught of resource extraction and attempts to "better" the landscape. The hand of man has never been light, especially when it comes to water in the arid and semi-arid western United States. In 1902, Senator Francis Newlands of Nevada, one of the primary authors of the Reclamation Act that was the legislative vehicle under which industrial-scale water development was initiated, cynically noted that "fish have no standing in water law," while attending the dedication of Derby Dam, which diverted the waters of the Truckee River from Pyramid Lake and its unique Lahontan cutthroat trout population.[57]

Most Americans in the late nineteenth century and early twentieth century viewed natural resources almost exclusively through the prism of exploitation. Like the harvest of forests for timber and the overgrazing of desert, sagebrush steppe, and mountain valleys, water was seen as "worthless" until put to better use for industrial economic benefit. This worthlessness of water was codified in western water law, which viewed water as beneficial only if it was first put into service through irrigation for agriculture, placed behind dams to pass through turbines to supply hydropower, or harvested for other industrial uses. The individual who first diverted water from its channel or pulled it from the depths of a pond or lake was the only one entitled to that water, and the earlier this was accomplished, the more entrenched the stake; thus was born the phrase "first in time, first in right," which is often bandied about in discussions of western water law. In the West, probably the only phrase about water better known is "whiskey is for drinking, water is for fighting." Both speak to the importance of water in shaping the industries and culture of the western United States.

Western water law is the child born of the labors of miners and farmers and their efforts to subjugate western lands, as they set about working the territories of the post–Civil War western states.[58] A direct rejection of the egalitarian riparian doctrine of the states east of the Mississippi River, western water law early on established the privatization of a public natural resource.[59] In this paradigm, there is no room for trout or their habitat, as so poignantly noted by Senator Newlands. Western water law has resulted in an overappropriation of waters across the western United States and serves as the legal basis for continued degradation of aquatic ecosystems. This single paragraph does no justice to the intricacies, idiosyncrasies, and nuances of western water law, nor does it speak to the institution's importance to the economic and cultural fabric of the western states. But it must not go unrecognized that western water law is often a barrier to the protection and restoration of trout and their habitat, as tall as any dam along any western river.

As is probably clear by now, Yellowstone cutthroat trout are in some ways better off than many other western trout. Unlike many western trout—with the exception of the rainbow trout—Yellowstone cutthroat have been widely stocked outside of their native range. A fifty-seven-year fish culturing and hatchery operation established on the shore of Yellowstone Lake around 1900 eventually produced 818 million eggs for shipment and stocking for waters outside Yellowstone National Park and outside the native range of the Yellowstone cutthroat trout.[60] The stocking of the YCT outside of its native range has created management challenges for other native western trout, including the westslope cutthroat trout that is native to the waters of the Columbia River Basin. Nevertheless, Yellowstone cutthroat trout, like nearly every other trout native to the western United States, are in a vortex of ecological decline. Developing solutions to halt the ongoing decline begins with addressing the continued stocking of non-natives into still-occupied ranges of native trout. We must also evolve in our conservation support from wild fisheries to support native fisheries whenever possible, which means that some wild populations of non-natives must be removed to make room for a return of the natives.

CHAPTER 9

Bountiful Trout, Threatened Natives

I TOOK ADVANTAGE OF EVERY opportunity to explore the varied waters of New Hampshire during my tenure as a graduate student. On numerous occasions, I explored the venerable White Mountains and its Appalachian streams and rivers, and even more frequently, I took advantage of the public river access on the waters near the seacoast, including the Lamprey, Exeter, and Cocheco Rivers. But even with these New England rivers to explore, Rubyat called to me relentlessly, so much so that in 2008 my wife and I grabbed our miniature dachshund, Snickers, and drove from New Hampshire to Wyoming in order to spend a week within the cabin's cozy wooden walls.

When we stepped through the back door of the cabin and I looked around the hushed kitchen, it took a moment for my eyes to adjust, as shadows and dust swirled through the air. My glance finally settled on the massive wooden cabinet that held everything from dishes to cooking staples. The cabinet stood against the back wall of the kitchen as it always had—but something was amiss: it was no longer white! Someone had painted the wood of the seven-foot-tall cabinet a light coffee brown. Then I realized the old black-and-white-checkerboard linoleum had also been changed, replaced with a faux-wood pattern. I began to stalk through the cabin, documenting each change, with a slowly building sense of anger and dread. Thresholds and windowsills had been repainted! The tin that had always held fresh, cold spring water from up the road had been replaced by a dingy little plastic water cooler! When I opened the door to the porch and stepped through, I was struck by the ultimate insult: the swing was gone! Whipping around, I found that the venerable artifact had been relocated from the west corner of the porch to the east. It was still the same handmade wooden swing that my great-great-grandfather had constructed, and it hung from the same old rusty chains, but that seemed inconsequential. It was nothing short of a travesty that the swing had been moved; it was the ultimate desecration of a holy site! Clearly, our vacation was ruined. How could I possibly enjoy myself when surrounded by change—here, at what was supposed to be the never-changing center of my universe?

The vacation, fortunately, was salvaged by my wonderful wife, who was eventually able to soothe my injured senses. After she convinced me to look at each change a little more closely, I had to grudgingly admit that some were well intentioned. The old black-and-white linoleum had been in terrible shape, even when I was a child. I couldn't accept the new water cooler, but I managed to locate the missing water tin on a cabinet out on the porch and return it to its rightful place in the cabin, banishing the plastic cooler to the darkest corner of the porch I could find.

That evening, I also began to appreciate why the holy relic that is the swing had been moved. When I walked over to the spot where it had hung my entire life, I realized that the small grove of evergreens from my childhood had grown tall enough to obscure the meadow behind their expanding boughs, blocking the view. When I walked to the opposite end of the porch and joined my wife on the swing, I realized we were now able to gaze into the meadow from this new vantage point. And while the scene that stretched before was much the same as it had been in my youth, filled with meadow grasses, wildflowers, willows, and lodgepole pines, the role each of these played suddenly also appeared different to me, as I now was able to see them through the prism of an ecologist. I realized that Rubyat's lesson for me this visit would be a lesson about how difficult—and necessary—it is to adjust to change.

WILD VS. NATIVE

Envisioning change, let alone actively seeking it out, is unfamiliar territory for most people, no less so when it comes to rehabilitating the waters and landscapes we love. One of the most difficult discussions bedeviling cold-water fishery conservation is that of wild versus native species management. The discussion encompasses whether or not coldwater conservation—in this case, trout conservation—should support wild fisheries or native fisheries. This raises the question of the difference between the terms *wild* and *native* and what this distinction ultimately means for trout conservation throughout the waters of the Rocky Mountains and beyond. Wild fisheries are waters in which non-native species have been stocked outside their native range and have since established self-sustaining populations. Native trout are those that have evolved in the landscape in which we find them.

Cold and warm waters alike have faced an ecological onslaught as non-native fish have been stocked outside their native ranges. Wild non-native trout have descended from stocks that were raised in a hatchery before being planted into waters outside their home range. As is often the case when a species is introduced into a new high-quality habitat, these planted trout have thrived and reproduced for many generations, producing a population that may or may not closely reflect the hatchery stock from which they are descended (although it is also the case that many times stocked species have failed to colonize what would appear to be ideal habitat).

Wild trout populations have received a considerable amount of attention from both the sport-angling and conservation communities. Among those who pursue trout with rod and reel, wild trout are believed to be more wary and wily and therefore better quarry for pursuit than hatchery-raised trout. Trout dumped by buckets from a truck into a waterway are seen as prey only for the lazy and uninitiated. As Anders Halverson has documented in his work, hatcheries over the course of generations have crossed and recrossed various strains of trout to produce what the sporting public has wanted: trout that fight harder and are more elusive—and therefore more desirable as angling quarry.

Support for wild populations has also received considerable attention from the conservation community. One of the most obvious reasons is that there is a fair amount of overlap between the conservation community and the angling community. These two constituencies also provide a feedback loop between themselves and the state game and fish agencies that are responsible for fishery management.

A perceived benefit of wild fisheries is the belief that if they are properly managed, they are sustainable. This requires that harvest be limited, and in many cases, the type of tackle used on such waters restricted, in order to reduce hooking mortality of fish that are returned to the water in catch-and-release fisheries. Support for catch-and-release fisheries has resulted in tension, however, between fly fishers and other fishing communities, including those who fish with spin tackle that relies on spoons, lures, and treble hooks, but even more so with those who fish for trout with live bait. Behnke, after reviewing the literature on hooking mortality and special regulations in his regular column in Trout Unlimited's *Trout* magazine, very forcefully laid out the case that while the type of artificial tackle and hook is irrelevant to the mortality of fish in a catch-and-release fishery, fishing with live bait is accompanied by the highest degree of mortality.[61] What this tells us is that the friction that commonly arises between fly fishers and other light-tackle enthusiasts is largely unnecessary but that there is a need to address the role of live bait within sport fishery policy, particularly on waters that are governed by catch-and-release special regulations or are being considered for such—which are, more often than not, well-established wild fisheries.

In many ways, the debate over wild versus native is an extension of the earlier conservation debate over wild versus hatchery-based fisheries. In this earlier debate, which continues to this day in many respects, a central point of contention was whether fisheries management should focus on providing anglers fishing opportunities through heavily stocking waters for the take of those trout or focus on managing habitat and self-sustaining wild populations. Behnke, in his discussion on the topic in the 1991 fall issue of *Trout* magazine, noted that 50 percent of hatchery-raised, catchable-sized stocked trout are caught by less than 10 percent of anglers.[62] He further noted that this has resulted in a disproportionate subsidy for a small group of the overall sport fishing population that pursue trout.[63]

Native fisheries can be, and in most cases are, wild fisheries, but in the parlance of trout management, the term *wild fishery* is typically reserved for waters containing stocked non-natives that have become self-sustaining. Instead, let us recognize *native fisheries* as those waters that are still occupied by the trout that have evolved within them. There are, in fact, cases where the natives that inhabit their historical habitat are stocked in order to maintain a native population—the Lahontan cutthroat trout of Pyramid Lake in Nevada, for instance.

If the question were simply one of managing for either wild non-native fisheries or native fisheries, management of many waters would be much more straightforward than it is today. But the issue is complicated by the fact that in many waters, including my home-waters, native populations continue to cling to existence in rivers, lakes, ponds, and tributaries, even as these waters continue to be stocked with non-natives. In some instances, stocking has ceased, but the non-natives have established wild self-sustaining populations that compete with natives. The question then becomes: wild or native? Although it makes sense to start by asking why both can't be sustained, the answer to that question is not always straightforward and often quite complex.

Making Room for Natives

The simple answer, at least on the surface, is that over a long enough timeline, non-natives will often outcompete and displace natives, ultimately driving the native trout to local extinction. If this is the case, then it may appear that the easy and sustainable solution is to conserve the native fishery through the cessation of non-native stocking and the removal of those species that have been stocked or have become self-sustaining.

The cessation of non-native stocking is certainly a start to the preservation of native fisheries. However, it is challenging to attempt to remove brown, brook, lake, and rainbow trout that have become established in waters outside of their native range.[64] If the waters are small enough—for example, small tributaries and mountain streams— non-native trout can be removed by a number of means. First, it may be possible to encourage anglers to fish the waters hard enough to pull most of the non-natives from the water and take them home for dinner, although that has become a more difficult prospect culturally, as the catch-and-release ethic has spread; there also exists a great deal of uncertainty about whether fishing pressure is enough to remove the vast majority of non-natives even in small waters. Second, game and fish agencies can use equipment to shock the waters, stunning fish so that they can be swept up with a net, placed in buckets, and taken to new waters. Then there are physical and biological controls, including introducing predators, changing streamflows, and introducing or removing barriers.[65] Finally, lethal methods can be used to remove trout from the waters. This is most commonly accomplished using a piscicide known as rotenone that is dispersed into water through the use of drip lines or spray equipment. The poison affects gill-breathing organisms and poses no harm to humans or animals that feed upon the dead fish, but it does kill other aquatic species with gills including invertebrates and amphibians.[66]

Not surprisingly, the use of poison in freshwater is often met with stiff resistance from the general public. A great deal of effort has been made to inform the public of the limits of the poison and to demonstrate that there is no harm to humans as a result of its use. Steps are also taken to place a neutralizing agent in the form of potassium permanganate into the water and thereby limit the poison's effects beyond the physical scope of a project, even before it dilutes and dissipates naturally. But mistakes do happen, sometimes with awful consequences.

In his detailed account of how rainbow trout have become a ubiquitous species found throughout the coldwater environs of the world, Anders Halverson details how the Green River project spanning Wyoming and Utah was poorly conceived, poorly planned, and poorly executed. The plan was to use rotenone to poison the entirety of the stretch of the Green River and its tributaries between the then unfinished Flaming Gorge and Fontenelle Dams. All told, nearly 450 miles of the river and its tributaries were treated, removing all native species in order to make way for a trophy non-native fishery largely based on trout.[67] One of the justifications for the project was that the natives of the river would be lost following construction of the dams, as the warm-water fishery would be transformed into a coldwater tailwater fishery, with water being released from the bottom of the reservoirs—so why not take advantage of the situation by speeding the process along and create an economically beneficial non-native fishery through stocking at the same time?

In preparation for the project, biologists and natural resource managers from state and federal agencies prepared and positioned the equipment and chemicals necessary to execute the plan. The spigots opened on September 4, 1962, and the release of the poison went on for three full days. A series of unforeseen troubles plagued the project from that moment on. In short, the biologists lost control of the project, were unable to neutralize the poison downstream as planned, and the poison made its way into Dinosaur National Monument. While proponents of the project claimed there was no way to tell if the dead fish found within the boundaries of the monument had been poisoned there or had simply floated downstream, the public didn't care about the distinction. Outrage over the seemingly careless operation was widespread, and natural resource managers paid a high price for the Green River project, as Rachel Carson's book *Silent Spring*, which was released nearly simultaneously, called to the public's attention the toll paid for the indiscriminate use of toxins in the environment.[68]

As fishery management and aquatic ecology have matured, a shift in the use of rotenone has taken place. Although the poison is now used to remove non-natives in support of protecting and expanding the range of native species, mistakes do still occur occasionally. One example is the loss of a population of native Bonneville cutthroat trout in Salt Lake City, Utah, when biologists used rotenone to remove rainbow trout upstream of the population but ended up decimating the cutthroat trout population they sought to protect.[69] Mistakes can and will happen and should not be used as an excuse to prevent future beneficial projects from taking place, but neither should it be expected that the public will necessarily accept the use of rotenone without thorough engagement or without complaint. Careful consideration must be given to the use of the poison and the tradeoffs carefully weighed and communicated to the public, which includes the potential for an accident, the potential scale of an accident, and a response plan.

Separately or combined, trout removal efforts may successfully remove wild non-native trout from waters, allowing for the expansion of a still existing native population or the reintroduction of extirpated natives. But there is a physical limitation to these methods of fish removal because there are a large number of waters where there is currently no technologically available means of removing non-natives from the waters and restoring native populations.

There are also social issues to be considered along with the ecological implications of purging wild trout waters to restore natives. The main stems of the Yellowstone River and the Bighorn River, for example, are world-renowned, blue-ribbon trout waters, and any plans to purge them would likely receive a great deal of pushback from the sport-angling community, as well as from the guides and business owners who have a vested interest in maintaining the non-native wild fishery.

In many instances, game and fish agencies, in combination with conservation groups, have begun the arduous task of returning natives to their home ranges within the Rocky Mountains. Agencies employ the techniques discussed above, focusing on waters that are amenable, given the physical limitations of the techniques and the budgetary constraints of the agencies and their partners. In order for such a strategy to succeed, a physical barrier must exist somewhere along the waterways to prevent non-natives from moving from their stronghold into the recently purged waters. This, however, creates a new ecological difficulty for the expansion or reintroduction of natives. Barriers, either natural or man-made, that prevent non-natives from again colonizing and displacing newly established natives also prevent native species from expanding their range to waters occupied by wild non-natives. Barriers also keep native populations physically separated from one another and therefore deny the species the opportunity to exchange genes (which is an important factor in maintaining a healthy population) or to colonize waters where ecological disturbance has opened habitat for recolonization. For example, a wildfire may wash sediment and debris into a stream, delivering the killing blow to a population that was just hanging on, since one disturbance event may be all it takes for a population to be rendered extinct that has already seen its numbers diminished as a result of numerous stresses. Any barrier that keeps out non-natives would also prevent natives from recolonizing this portion of their historical range and reestablishing a population. Thus we can see some of the difficulties associated with trying to maintain or develop a native fishery when a wild non-native fishery is in place.

RAINBOW TROUT & HYBRIDIZATION

Rainbow trout and cutthroat trout have been geologically separated and genetically diverging from one another for nearly two million years, following an ancestral split during the Pliocene epoch.[70] This physical separation has not been long enough, however, to prevent interbreeding between the two species when they are once again placed within the same waters. This is yet another means through which wild non-natives put native trout populations at risk through continued stocking.

Hybridization of non-native rainbow with native cutthroat trout is a pervasive and widespread problem in waters throughout the western United States. While specific populations of rainbow and cutthroat trout have evolved sympatrically in the same waters, resulting in evolutionary tactics to maintain genetic integrity (such as the use of different spawning habitats, even though they respond to the same spawning cues),[71] evolutionary mechanisms such as these are not in place for the vast majority of waters in which cutthroat trout populations are native and hatchery-raised rainbow trout are, or were, stocked. The result is hybridization between rainbow trout and cutthroat trout that undermines the genetic integrity of the native population with a multitude of associated negative consequences. Hybridization and the conservation of native trout populations, however, reach well beyond simply rainbow and cutthroat trout. For example, the bull trout of the Columbia River Basin, listed as threatened under the Endangered Species Act, can interbreed with introduced brook trout that have been stocked within the bull trout's native range.[72]

Of course, there are exceptions to every rule. Coastal cutthroat trout have coevolved throughout the entirety of their range with rainbow trout and have developed the necessary evolutionary traits to maintain reproductive isolation and therefore preclude hybridization between the two species in most cases.[73] Nevertheless, the introduction of hatchery-propagated rainbow trout (as opposed to native populations of rainbow trout) can undermine the evolutionary traits that have been developed over eons to maintain genetic purity between the two species, resulting in hybridization between native coastal cutthroat trout and the hatchery-raised fish.[74] It is also interesting to note that, to a much lesser extent, the westslope cutthroat trout of the Columbia River Basin coevolved with rainbow trout and redband trout in select drainages and have managed to maintain their genetic integrity, but as with coastal cutthroat trout, the introduction of hatchery-raised rainbow trout has led to hybridization between the two.[75]

Perhaps the foremost concern related to the hybridization of native and non-native species is the loss of genetic integrity of the native trout populations that have evolved over millennia to survive and thrive within their native habitat. In the case of rainbow trout and cutthroat trout, as well as bull trout and brook trout crosses, the hybrid offspring that result are capable of producing fertile offspring themselves, resulting in a further dilution of native genetic integrity, as well as continually expanding populations of hybridized trout. Over the course of generations, continued interbreeding between natives, non-natives, and hybrids can result in a "hybrid swarm."[76] What this means is that every offspring of a hybrid is a hybrid and that genetic purity can only increasingly suffer. The continued interbreeding of hybrids and non-natives has been found by researchers to undermine the fitness of native species even within their native habitat, putting their survival as a species at stake.[77]

Non-natives that have been stocked outside their native range prove problematic for native species, whether the non-natives have established a wild population or not. When comparing the ease with which the different species of trout can be caught, cutthroat trout are the most susceptible to the trickery of hook and fly, followed by brook trout, rainbow trout, and then brown trout, which are the most wily.[78] What this means for native cutthroat trout in waters where non-natives have been stocked is that, as a result of their willingness to take a fly, cutthroat trout are more likely to be caught and taken home for dinner, if not released back into the water. But even if a trout is released, there is always the chance that it will succumb to the trauma of being caught and landed, ultimately resulting in its death. Even if a stream has catch-and-release regulations, cutthroat trout are in danger of being removed from their native waters when those waters are also occupied by non-natives, as a result of hooking mortality. In turn, the habitat that is made available as a result of the disproportionate catching of natives is then filled with non-natives that may or may not be hybridizing and further undermining the native trout population. Take this difficult ecological situation and add to it the intentional breeding, stocking, and promotion of hybridized species such as the cutbow (cutthroat x rainbow trout cross) and we begin to see how stocking of non-natives into the waters of native species can dramatically threaten what remains of native species populations.

Beware Homogenization

Difficulties in the debate between wild versus native fisheries extend beyond sport-angling and conservation groups to state agencies charged with managing game and fish. I traveled home to the Greater Yellowstone Ecosystem to interview natural resource managers for my master's thesis work on the policy surrounding Yellowstone cutthroat trout, while the species was being considered for listing under the Endangered Species Act. During a wonderfully candid discussion, a manager there confided to me that people in his own department often confused the issue of wild versus native fisheries by conflating the two terms. This conflation of terminology leads to an even greater challenge when it comes to informing and educating the public, as well as garnering support for both wild and native fishery programs and projects.

The root of this discussion is built on the history and legacy of those who have come before us as fishery managers, conservationists, and anglers. It would be easy, and an egregious mistake, to attempt to blame managers and stakeholders of the late nineteenth and early twentieth centuries for the current predicament of native species loss and expansion of non-natives throughout the United States. The attitudes of fish and wildlife managers, biologists, and educated folk involved in the development of fish culture and propagation were a reflection of their times. During this era, it was widely believed that nature needed a human hand to truly thrive. Whether this was the result of an increased recognition of the impacts of an industrialized nation on its natural resources or simply an overly optimistic belief in the benign ability of humans to "improve" upon nature, I don't know. But I do know that we cannot condemn our predecessors for reflecting the society of which they were a part. Relitigating the past only diverts attention from the conservation needs of the present.

Our coldwater fisheries are under assault from many directions, of which self-sustaining wild non-native populations are only a single—but, I believe, an ecologically outsized—facet. Habitat loss and fragmentation, pollution, and climate change all combine to push our native species into smaller and smaller territories and waters. In many ways, it is because of these multi-pronged threats that I so fully support the transition from a wild-based to a native-based conservation strategy. Our stocking efforts have ensured that brook, brown, lake, and rainbow trout will thrive in the Rocky Mountains and beyond, but it is far less certain that this is true of many of our western native species. Transitioning from a wild to a native conservation strategy will require that we ask the hard question of what we truly want from our recreation experience. Is it enough to cast a fly on resplendent waters surrounded by jagged mountain peaks and verdant forests? Or do we want the opportunity to catch a native of the very landscape that we either inhabit or purposefully sought out in order to pursue trout? Personally, I want to pass on a natural resource heritage to my children that includes the ability to fish the same waters I did growing up, surrounded by the same beauty, while also knowing that the fish they catch are a reflection of the land in which they are fishing. Undoubtedly there will always be waters in the Rocky Mountains that will hold populations of non-natives, whether stocked or wild, but our goal should be to preserve our natives and their habitat whenever and wherever possible. In this way, native trout could become the twenty-first-century inheritors of the conservation efforts that developed, and were so successful, in maintaining and improving habitat for wild trout in the twentieth century.

Up to this point, we have largely considered native trout in the context of individual species and populations, but the plight of native trout is a reflection of changes that are taking place on a global scale. We are entering an era of modern extinction on the scale of the five historical mass extinctions that have reordered life throughout the world.[79] The human species has become a force of nature that is actively reshaping the natural world, and the ongoing mass extinction of what has been termed the "Anthropocene era" is a symptom of human domination of the biosphere. In addition to the loss of countless species, we are facing the dangers of homogenization, as species are being rapidly moved outside their native ranges: mammals, reptiles, amphibians, fish, plants, insects, bacteria, and viruses have all been transported across mountain ranges, between watersheds, and over oceans to take up residence in new habitats, usually at the expense of native species. In short, we are on the verge of losing the biodiversity that has, in the past, made a region, mountain range, or even a lake special; instead, each place will become just like any other place, with only a local change of scenery.

The stocking of non-native trout plays a role in this homogenization. As we allow non-natives to continue to be stocked in our favorite waters and as the natives of our home-waters retreat to smaller and smaller parcels of habitat, we rob ourselves and those who follow us of a significant natural and cultural heritage. We may feel secure in our ability to seek out and cast to a native trout in our lifetime, but if species continue to succumb to this latest great extinction, can the same be said for our grandchildren and their grandchildren? If we want to stave off the looming coldwater ecological disaster that would result from the loss of native trout, we must promote significant change not only in our fishery policies but also in the ecosystems surrounding them.

Part II

CHAPTER 10

Beyond the Streambanks

WHEN I WAS A CHILD, two evergreen trees stood as spiny sentinels to the open meadow below the cabin, marking the nearest edge of the glade. Throughout the years of my absence from the cabin during high school and college, the evergreens grew large and gruff, neglecting their grassy charge. By the time I returned in 2003, the meadow had been filled in with willows, and new trees had taken root in solitary locations throughout. During that visit, when I entered the diminished meadow, it was only by following the path mostly by memory, around the pine sentinels and skirting the tallest willows, that I was able to find my way back to the rock island.

In my absence, Time and his mistress, Mother Nature, had laid their hands on the rock island, just as they had on the meadow, the trees, and the stream itself. No longer was the island just a heap of loosely piled stones. Rushing flows from springtime snowmelt had reshaped the it, stacking more and more rocks upon its cobbled surface; those same rushing waters had reshaped the channel itself. The deep pool at the head of the rock island still existed, but water now ran past it through a narrowed gap into a second, shallower pool that had previously been a deep trough, too deep to wade safely when I was ten years old. When I was young and fished the rock island, the majority of water flowed through the deep trough passing in front of the island and ran toward the meandering bend downstream, but that was no longer the case. The waters of Tensleep Creek had since shifted, as the stream channel at the bottom edge of the rock island had become clogged with rocks and the remnants of undercut banks that had lost their integrity and fallen into the stream. The result was that most of the water was directed away from the rock island, rather than around it, and down to the meandering bend that had served as my childhood fishing boundary.

When I looked across the stream, I realized that the beaver dam no longer spanned the two distant banks; instead, the stream sparkled as it passed into tree-cast shadows and turned quickly behind a thicket before disappearing from sight. Although I mourned the loss of the beaver dam, I had never thoroughly explored the area behind the dam, and now the darkly glittering waters seemed newly inviting. I returned to the cabin to unpack and get something to eat, intent on returning quickly with fly rod in hand.

Standing on the porch, a cold sandwich in my hand, I watched as rain began to fall lightly. Hunger had pulled me from the water, but the light rain bode well for the evening's fishing. The rain, however, began to fall in bigger drops, and the sound of rain on the tin roof reverberated throughout the entire cabin, accentuating the power of the storm. As the skies opened up, the rain beat down upon the roof, until the force of the falling rain eventually muffled all other sounds beneath the storm's onslaught. Never before had I seen so much rain fall in such a short span of time in the Bighorn Mountains. The rain just as quickly came to an end, filling the surrounding forest with a heavy silence. I decided to not return to the stream that evening, opting instead to enjoy my sandwich from the vantage point of the porch swing, where I could watch the forest around me come back to life after the storm.

RETURN OF THE MOOSE

During the Johnson family reunion when I was ten years old, I had taken a walk with my father, who at the time I barely knew, down the two-track road that leads to the cabin. Making our way past the other cabins on the rutted road, we passed by the meadow that I frequently crossed on my way to the stream. We skirted its far edge, watching as the grassy field became wetter, and then as grass gave way to willows that were divided in many places by open water.

After hopping across the inches-deep Bear Creek that bisected the road, we climbed the last hill before returning to the well-maintained Forest Service road. When we paused at the crest of the hill and looked down into the willows and water at this end of what had been the meadow, my father warned me to never fish in the open waters below us, since the water in the pools was stagnant; eating the flesh of fish caught within them would make me sick. I turned from the sight wistfully, as I watched concentric circles gently drift across the surface of the small pools, following the soft pluck of an insect from the surface by a resident trout. My father's timely warning was enough to keep me from ever wetting my line in the abundant ponds below the hill.

I would later recognize that abundant beaver activity was the underlying cause of the many pools that I was forbidden to fish as a child. Beavers had dammed the waters of Bear Creek that crossed the road, adding to the flooding of the already saturated soils and allowing juvenile trout to maintain happy lives within the seemingly motionless waters. Over the years, the character of the ponds behind the small beaver dams and the dispersed willows changed, in much the same way that the meadow itself had slowly transformed. As the lodgepole pine trees below the cabin reached ever upward, spreading their cone- and needle-filled limbs wider, the open waters of the ponds slowly dwindled until they disappeared altogether.

Sediment and detritus slowly filled the shallow pools, while willows continued to grow, flourish, and spread. Over the course of years, the pools filled in, such that the vast majority of open water behind the miniature beaver dams disappeared, leaving behind an arterial-like branching of small rivulets. Many of these streamlets simply disappeared into the wet, saturated soils; others would add their tiny flow of water to the minute trickles of others, eventually making their way to Tensleep Creek itself. Left behind was a patchwork of thick willows, wet soils, black pools of water, and numerous pits, in which an unwary angler could stumble and find himself up to his knees in icy water when trying to push his way through the copse.

A second change had taken place in conjunction with the transition of the beaver ponds to willow thickets: moose—an animal that had been absent from the meadows and the streambanks below the cabin during my youth—had returned. I would later learn that they favored the willow thickets that had sprung up upon the once nearly stagnant beaver ponds and the patches of willows that had grown to largely encircle the meadow I had tramped across as a child. At the time of my visit in 2003, though, I didn't realize that the prevalence of beavers and the return of the moose were most likely intertwined. Although I had been warned by my grandfather that moose had returned to the area and liked to inhabit the willows, my first encounter with moose would not be in the meadow but on the creek upstream from the cabin.

Subalpine fir encroaching on the edge of the stream towered invitingly in the afternoon heat. I was happy to find respite within their cool shade, as the sun beat down on a cloudless summer day. While it is impossible to do justice to the stunning azure canvas of a summer's day in the Bighorn Mountains, the heat of this day was enough to make me wish for a summer thunderstorm to provide a little sweet relief. The streamside path was clear and well beaten into the terrain, crossing beneath lodgepole pines, through a small grove of tall willows, and over downed tree trunks that lay gray and rotting on the ground. I continued on the path, passing by the boulder where Grandpa had stood with me to catch my first fish, until I found an open spot with easy access to the stream.

On this sublime summer day, I was wearing shorts rather than my typical denim jeans, so I decided to slide from the bank into the water, pausing as its chill flow swept over my feet and bare legs, which were still pasty white from the previous winter. I could see that there were potential trout-holding waters on both sides of the bank. As I slowly made my way to the center of the stream, crystal-clear water swirled up to my knees but no higher. I slid my feet carefully from cobble to cobble, since the old tennis shoes I was wearing were hardly conducive to aquatic travel.

Shuffling my way upstream beneath the shadows of the subalpine firs, I cast to each side of the creek. The gaudy Hornberg fly that I had tied to the end of my tippet drifted high on the water, passing from shadow to light, picking up speed as it neared the bank. Occasionally a dark shape would dart toward the garish mouthful from beneath tree roots exposed within the last season or two of high water. A small splash and the flash of white and orange told me that a brook trout had tried to catch my fly skittering across the water's surface.

Maybe it was the heat of the day or maybe the Hornberg was a bit too much, but the strikes were few and far between. I came to a bend that seemed to be a good spot to exit the water and tie on a new fly. Reeling in my loose line, I turned toward the bank and was stopped dead in my tracks. Less than five feet from me stood a cow moose on the bank with her head thrust through a sheaf of willow branches. Staring at me with disdain, she took a massive bite of the apparently succulent leaves and soft willow twigs and chewed leisurely, never taking her big brown eyes from me. Without reeling any further, I slowly shuffled my way across the stream to the opposite bank. Apparently neither I nor my fly rod were intimidating; by the time I had stepped onto the opposite bank, she had decided I wasn't even worth watching anymore and instead turned her full attention to the meal at hand. Pulling myself onto the bank, I quickly made my way further upstream, leaving the moose to her peaceful summertime meal.

Since that first encounter, I've had many more run-ins with the moose that inhabit the forest, meadows, and waters around the cabin. Each year I've been able to add a new moose-related story to my collection. There was the time when my wife caught *her* first fish—as I charged out of the stream to congratulate her and help her remove the fish from her line, I spooked a young moose out of the willow thicket next to her. And there was the time our ten-pound miniature dachshund chased a moose from the stream's edge, past the cabin, and deep into the forest. I'm convinced the moose never knew how little the beast was that was making all the racket behind it or it would have turned around and given my little dog the what-for. But all turned out well; I was able to convince little Snickers to come back, the moose retreated into the forest, and I was spared from having to explain to my wife how I had lost our dog to a moose.

Unbeknownst to me during my first encounter with the moose along the stream, moose are not native to the Bighorn Mountains. The moose that have colonized the riparian areas of Tensleep Creek are likely the descendants of eight moose (six females and two males) that were introduced to the mountain range on May 27, 1948. Since that initial transplant, a number of additional transplants have been made into the Bighorn Mountains. From what I have been able to discern, all the moose relocated to the Bighorns were first captured near Jackson Hole, Wyoming.[80]

Ecosystem Engineers

Growing up, I was forbidden to head downstream from the rock island toward the beaver dam that spanned one branch of the stream that split as it flowed past the island. I don't recall ever seeing the productive tenants working near or around their well-built structure, but the dam was maintained for many years. Any remnants of the beaver's hard work on the dam have been lost, as the dam has been swept away with the change in the stream's course around the rock island. But there are still some signs of their handiwork that have been captured on the landscape.

The beaver's engineering was evident throughout the riparian areas on Tensleep Creek. Where once there were sizable, nearly stagnant pools of water harboring the trout I was expressly told not to pursue, the area has since been transformed into a large, dense willow thicket, and it's likely that the influence of resident beavers didn't end there. It is also quite possible that part of the reason moose have moved into the region is a result of the beaver's handiwork.

Moose are browsers—that is to say, their preferred food consists of the branches, stems, and leaves of shrubs and trees, of which willow is a favorite. Willow has always inhabited portions of the streambank: in open areas between evergreen trees, in flat expanses of wet meadow, and in stretches of open terrain on the inside of oxbows in the areas below the cabin. The damming of the small trickles of water from feeder streams led, over time, to the gradual filling in of small channels and holes with nutrient-rich sediment, allowing willows to expand to new areas and to thicken and grow taller where they were already established. Water from feeder streams still manages to make its way to the creek, but it is no longer impounded behind small beaver dams. In many areas, the water follows narrow channels to join the streams, but just as often, it saturates the soil and travels beneath the surface. I have to tread carefully when working my way from one fishing spot to the next through this area, since the surface in many places is quite soft and water very near the surface. Every step brings with it the possibility of losing a poorly tied shoe in the pull of black, slurping mud. The deeper water hidden behind and beneath large tangles of willow branches and the roots overlaying sandy bottom pools provide refuge for small trout to lurk and snatch tiny insects from above and below the water, until the trout grow large enough to join their kin in the main stream channel.

To the naked eye, the beaver's industrious products have long since vanished, but the legacy of their activities is still stamped on the landscape below the family cabin. The expansion of the willows around the meadow below the cabin has provided a belt of tall vegetation that stretches from the hillside to the edge of the stream, heads downstream for a considerable distance, and then continues on the opposite bank to such an extent that only the foolish travel through it. This expanse of willow has provided a perfect haven for moose.

The area, while not overly large, provides a plethora of benefits as a result of the industrious beaver's labor. Beavers have been hailed as ecosystem engineers for their ability to reshape the landscape; their industry certainly has provided benefits to the moose. The damming that led to the establishment of a wet meadow and a willow-shrub riparian corridor provides the largest member of the deer family shade during hot summer days, as well as food. The thick cover also serves as a means of protective cover for newborn moose. Although two predators of the moose, the wolf and grizzly bear, no longer pose significant threats (grizzlies are no longer found in the Bighorn Mountains, and wolves exist in such small numbers as to be currently ecologically irrelevant), the willows provide concealment from other predators, such as black bears and occasionally mountain lions. Cascading ecological influences such as these are what make the ecosystem engineering impacts of the beaver so important.

Beavers work and reside in the riparian corridors that are the interface between the aquatic and upland terrestrial portions of the ecosystem. Riparian areas are valuable habitat for both fish and wildlife—which is kind of an odd distinction, if you think about it. Riparian areas contribute to the health of both the aquatic and nearby upland habitats.[81] In forest ecosystems like that of the Bighorn Mountains where the family cabin and my home-waters are located, beaver activities expand wetlands that provide a variety of benefits: increasing habitat for fish and macroinvertebrates, recharging ground water, elevating the water table, and stabilizing streambanks.[82]

As true ecosystem engineers, beavers reshape the vegetative diversity and abundance of trees and shrubs in the local area of their work, as a result of their feeding and building activities. When it comes to impacts on trout specifically, context is important, as is so often the case in nature. Depending on the size and location of a beaver dam and its pond, the work of beavers can either be a benefit to trout or a detriment.[83] There are a number of variables that influence the direct benefits of beaver activity to trout, including stream size, location of the dam, spawning and migration requirements of the trout species, life cycle of the trout species, preferred prey, and so on. Although the impacts of beaver activity may not be obvious and may not even provide a direct benefit that results in more or larger trout, if the ecosystem is not overly degraded, you can be sure that beavers are providing a benefit to the aquatic and surrounding upland areas of the ecosystem.

THE DYNAMIC RIPARIAN ZONE

The ecological benefit of beaver activities expands well beyond the immediate area of their dam and lodge, providing otherwise ignorant humans insight into just how broad and complex ecology can be. Occasionally, when the activities encroach on humans and our own ecosystem engineering activities, the work of beavers is seen as a nuisance. Appreciating the seemingly mundane daily activities of the beaver and their wide-ranging impacts allows us to recognize why it is important to protect aspects of our landscape that we don't necessarily understand or that we take for granted. The beavers below the cabin have provided a readily observable example of the complex relationships that comprise an ecosystem; just because we can't easily see the interconnections between other species doesn't mean they are not there.

The benefits of that narrow band known as the riparian zone, which is the interface between the aquatic home of trout and the uplands, cannot be overstated. Riparian zones are dynamic, highly diverse structures, in the form of grasses, shrubs, and trees that grow within the zone, and they are quite often more diverse than the surrounding uplands themselves.[84] This diversity of habitat likewise creates a diversity of wildlife, much of which directly or indirectly influences the aquatic environment (as well as the trout therein—and those of us who are anglers are often the beneficiaries when attempting to imitate terrestrial insects such as ants and beetles). Finally, the riparian zone directly influences streams and rivers by affecting the amount of sunlight that strikes the water's surface, by moderating water temperature, and by providing woody debris that makes its way into the channel and creates habitat complexity and cover for trout and, in some cases, refuge from predation.[85]

Over the years, I have come to appreciate the riparian zone both for its aesthetic value as well as for its ecosystem properties. While I have enjoyed watching the moose and occasional deer within the willows along the stream, as well as the numerous bird species that I have yet to learn to identify, it is the role the riparian zone plays in the overall health of my home-waters that I have most recently come to appreciate. Even though my gaze is often fixed on the surface of the water I'm fishing, I try to make it a point to look up and take in the surrounding lands and recognize that they influence the habitat of the trout that I'm pursuing . . . even if I'm busy extricating a fly snagged in a willow at the same time.

CHAPTER 11

A Howl in the Darkness

I WAS ON THE STREAM in the softening daylight, casting to rising trout as the sun filtered through the long shadows of lodgepole pines, while Grandma was hard at work preparing dinner. The gentle murmuring of the stream was punctuated by the periodic sound of trout rising to catch winged morsels from atop the water's surface. Between delicate dimpling of the water was the occasional unceremonious smack of my fly line on water, as I cast my dry fly pattern to the trout rising to consume some of the same mosquitoes that were buzzing mercilessly around my head.

The *rang-a-lang-a-lang* of metal on metal chimed through the mountain air from the triangle hung outside the front door of the cabin, alerting me to dinnertime. Dinner was always a full, well-cooked meal, even though the cabin was outfitted with all the conveniences of a mountain cabin built in 1916—which meant no running water, no electricity, and no heat other than what was provided through the burning of wood. Grandma would spend hours in front of the wood-burning stove as she prepared each meal, with the vast majority of that time spent stoking the fires within its cast-iron belly, until the plates resting on the stovetop were hot enough to cook upon. After having stoked the fire to the requisite temperature, she would pull together the necessary ingredients and produce the finest of meals under the most austere of circumstances.

After hearing the call of the metal triangle, I immediately reeled in my line and hoofed it across the meadow and up the hill to the cabin. After taking off my wet tennis shoes, I ran in the back door and was greeted by the smell of woodsmoke and spaghetti sauce. What young man could have resisted such a temptation after a day on the water? I quickly washed my hands in the basin tucked behind the door, then took a seat at the stout pine-wood dining table in the great room.

The behemoth stove was then, and is still now, one of the icons of the family cabin: the center around which activity often hums. I've been told the walls of the cabin were assembled after having first winched the massive iron beast into place with block-and-tackle and horses. Adjoining the kitchen is the great room, which is similarly dominated by a fireplace assembled from river rock. The great room is situated such that the river-rock hearth and chimney have been built upon a massive boulder, whose bulk beneath the ground is unknown but has served for over one hundred years as the unwavering foundation for the fireplace. In many ways, the cast-iron stove and the fireplace, along with its foundational boulder, are the physical anchors of Rubyat.

If the cast-iron stove and the river-rock fireplace are the foundational anchors of the cabin, the hand-carved porch swing is its heart. Hanging in the west corner of the porch, the swing overlooks the meadow below the cabin. Generations of my family have spent countless hours swaying back and forth on the swing as the old rusted chain gently creaks overhead. From the swing, a Norman Rockwell–like scene of forest, stream, and mountain meadows stretches before the onlooker, offering bucolic tranquility.

Like the entire cabin, the dining table and its chairs were handcrafted by my great-great-grandfather. Fashioned from lodgepole pine logs split by axe, maul, and chisel, the pine table stretches across the entire back wall of the great room, filling the space between the threshold leading to the kitchen and the threshold leading to the only bedroom. The chairs are crafted from smaller logs and branches; the sanded golden wood glows with an inner warmth that seems to welcome all to take a seat and enjoy the evening.

When we took our seats that evening, we were sitting at a table that had seen the joy of five generations' worth of family meals. Looking down from the walls around us were characters from the artwork of Philip Goodwin. Each scene is held in a frame constructed from the same local pine trees from which the table and chairs were fashioned; many are encased in individual split-wood frames that have maintained their thin, flaky bark nearly a century after the artwork was placed inside.

Each color print within the hand-carved pine-wood frames is a nature scene, and every scene contains the influence of man in one form or another, although not all are stamped with man's physical presence. When men are physically present in the scenes, they are not the hardscrabble migrants come to the Rockies in search of a homestead and a new life scratched from the frontier. No, the men in these scenes are well-groomed and well-dressed men of the upper echelon of society, testing their mettle in the wilderness. These are the men or the sons of the men who could have sat with Theodore Roosevelt as members of the earliest generations of the Boone and Crockett Club.

Our spaghetti dinner that night was quickly followed by the washing of dishes in water brought up from the stream and boiled appropriately. It was too dark by then to return to the stream, so Brandon and I changed into our pajamas and returned to the dining table. Evenings at the cabin could be spent as one pleased, which usually meant reading by the combined light of the fireplace and the gas lanterns, sitting around chatting, or playing family games. That night, Brandon and I decided we wanted to play Chinese checkers. It was a slow game but a great way to pass some time before roasting marshmallows on the end of willow switches in the stone fireplace.

Grandma, Grandpa, Brandon, and I each selected the color of marbles we wanted to use and placed them on the board. We were partway through our game when I first heard the howls coming from outside. I looked at Brandon and could tell that he heard the howls as well, but Grandpa and Grandma seemed not to take notice. Almost in unison, Brandon and I asked if the howling outside was wolves. With a chuckle, Grandpa informed us that there were no wolves left in these mountains and that it was only coyotes howling in the darkness. This reassurance was a huge relief to two little boys afraid of being eaten by wolves in the pitch black of night . . . and a tremendous disappointment to the ecologist one of those boys would become years later.

THE MISSING WOLVES

It would be overly simplistic to say that the calls we heard from inside the firelit cabin that summer evening could not have come from wolves because all the wolves in Wyoming had been killed decades earlier. To present the situation in such a simplistic fashion would veil over why the extermination had taken place, the cultural values that drove the policy, and the fact that, in a few short years after Brandon and I voiced the question to our grandparents, Wyoming would again see wolves within its borders. I would rather examine more closely some of the reasons why wolves were indeed extinct in the Bighorn Mountains the evening we asked that question of our grandparents and why that extinction was not the final curtain call for the species in Wyoming's mountains.

In their book *Wolves: Behavior, Ecology, Conservation*, L. David Mech and Luigi Boitani eloquently note that the reason wolves have been persecuted, often to the point of extinction at local and regional levels, is that throughout time they have competed with humans for resources.[86] Of course, the resource in question is food—for both species. The persecution of the wolf has, at times, been carried out under imperial authority, in the guise of a royal call to remove the species from the landscape.[87] At other times, the persecution has been carried out under the influence of religious decrees, as when the wolf was equated with sin and evil within Christianity.[88]

This low cultural value placed on the wolf crossed the Atlantic, from the Old World to the New, and a European value system that could condone the burning of Scotland's forests to eradicate the wolf found new life within the wilderness colonies in America.[89] As loss of habitat and competition for food increased, humans and wolves entered into a drawn-out battle that would push the wolf into remote corners of the country, even as its numbers continued to decline through perpetual persecution. As the United States expanded its boundaries under Manifest Destiny, humans and wolves would continue to act out the same drama across the American landscape.[90]

Some researchers have suggested that as American pioneers populated the Great Plains and pushed into the Rocky Mountains, the intentional devastation of the bison herds to support the policy of Native American subjugation may have resulted in a short-lived wolf population boom, as the wolves took advantage of the bounty supplied by the bison carcasses strewn across the Great Plains.[91] If the bison slaughter indeed resulted in an increase in wolf populations, it would ultimately prove to be to the long-term detriment of the wolf, as the Great Plains were repopulated with cattle.

Where once wolves and humans competed for wild game, the wolf would turn its attention to this new non-native form of prey that had replaced the bison that the wolf had evolved with on the landscape. The intensity of the backlash against wolves as a result of their preying on livestock would become an interest of the federal government, which would ultimately sanction the removal, by any means necessary, of wolves from their native ecosystems.[92] The use of poison, typically strychnine, would prove to be the most effective means of cheaply and efficiently removing wolves from lands believed to be better used for livestock grazing. The clout of the livestock industry would prove to be so strong that the national government became the chief persecutor of the wolf from 1915 until the enactment of the Endangered Species Act in 1973. The extensive program of wolf eradication even reached into some of the most protected corners of the United States—including Yellowstone National Park.

CALLS FOR COEXISTENCE

The preceding pages paint a somber picture of the interactions between wolves and humankind. But, again, it would be overly simplistic to regurgitate the destructive histories between humans and wolves without addressing the rapidly evolving debate (and actions) related to sharing the landscape. While undoubtedly the passing of the Endangered Species Act has played the key role in wolf restoration in the United States, a burgeoning call for coexisting with wolves began well before its enactment.

Aldo Leopold, an extraordinarily gifted ecologist, land ethicist, and writer, helped set the stage for coexistence. In *A Sand County Almanac*, first published in 1949, he described his experience after shooting a wolf on the side of a mountain:

> We reached the old wolf in time to watch a fierce green fire dying in her eyes. I realized then, and have known ever since, that there was something new to me in those eyes—something known only to her and the mountain. I was young then, and full of trigger-itch; I thought that because fewer wolves meant more deer, that no wolves would mean hunters' paradise. But after seeing the green fire die, I sensed that neither the wolf nor mountain agreed with such a view.[93]

Leopold would go on to advocate for the reintroduction of wolves to Yellowstone National Park.[94] Nearly seventy years later, contemporary ecologists, conservationists, and natural resource managers still look to Leopold's writings for guidance on wildlife management and ethics in natural resource management.

Originally signed into law in 1973, and amended a number of times since, the Endangered Species Act is the vehicle that has propelled gray wolf recovery in the United States. A year after the act became the national policy tool for species conservation, wolves were classified as endangered in Minnesota. In 1978 the gray wolf was classified as endangered throughout the lower forty-eight states, but it would not be until 1987 that a plan was put forth for the recovery of the species in the northern Rocky Mountains by the U.S. Fish and Wildlife Service.

The 1987 recovery plan set the stage for the reintroduction of wolves to Yellowstone National Park, as well as central Idaho, while supporting natural expansion of wolf populations in northwest Montana. It would be during the environmental review process of the potential environmental impacts associated with reintroduction that the antipathy between those who wanted to keep wolves out of Wyoming and those who wanted to see wolves reintroduced would be put on full and acrimonious display.

The National Environmental Policy Act of 1969 requires that major actions of the federal government be analyzed for their environmental impacts; the reintroduction of wolves to Yellowstone National Park and central Idaho was no exception. Over the course of two and a half years, 130 public meetings were held to gather public comments on the proposed reintroduction encapsulated in the environmental impact statement, resulting in 170,000 public comments.[95] As has proven to be the case with anything regarding wolves, emotions ran high. At one point during the process, Montana senator Conrad Burns claimed that a child would be dead within a year of reintroduction, in a highly charged attempt to bolster public opposition to gray wolf recovery.[96]

The return of the gray wolf to the Wyoming mountains began with the capture of wolves in Canada for later release.[97] The recovery process that began with the listing of the gray wolf as endangered in 1978 continued with the development of a recovery plan in 1987, which would see its first concrete steps toward success with the release of the captured gray wolves in 1995 and 1996. During the winter of 1995, fourteen wolves were released in Yellowstone National Park with a second release of seventeen wolves in 1996.

In the Rocky Mountains, the persecution, and by extension the recovery, of wolves is shrouded by an additional layer of complexity beyond the typical cultural preconceptions that prevent people from seeing the wolf for what it is—a wild animal with specific environmental requirements for survival; this additional layer is encompassed in the management of public lands and the role these lands play in the day-to-day lives of communities throughout the Rocky Mountains.

THE ROLE OF PUBLIC LANDS

Public lands are, in many ways, the economic lifeblood of the Intermountain West, an area that includes Wyoming and the Bighorn Basin. The U.S. Forest Service is one of four major public land management agencies that oversee activities across the public domain; the other three are the Bureau of Land Management, the National Park Service, and the U.S. Fish and Wildlife

Service. The Fish and Wildlife Service, in addition to being charged with the recovery of imperiled species, is also responsible for the management of the National Wildlife Refuge System throughout the United States.[98]

From the opening of the public domain for homesteading to the closing of the frontier in 1890, the management of public lands has always been politically charged. Historically, lands held in the public domain have been used for exploitation of their resources for economic gain. In addition to homesteading, forms of natural resource extraction, including logging, mining, oil and gas development, and agriculture have all been historical uses of public lands—uses that have been carried forward into the contemporary era.

Theodore Roosevelt may well have been one of the earliest proponents of natural resource conservation, albeit conservation viewed through the lens of pragmatism, as evidenced by his selection and support of Gifford Pinchot as his chief forester. Pinchot believed in treating forests as a form of agriculture and that the benefits of natural resource management should be viewed through the prism of the greatest good for the largest number of people possible. Nevertheless, President Roosevelt championed the conservation, and in some instances, protection, of natural resources, especially wildlife. The conservation ethic that developed during the Progressive Era continued to grow until it became a social movement capable of influencing national policy, as evidenced through environmental legislation that protected species and habitat and designated portions of public lands as wilderness.

Every designation of protection for public lands appeared to many who promoted public lands for economic gain as a direct challenge to the economic potential of the public domain and, by extension, the economic health of the United States. In the minds of many, it has been a zero-sum game: there could only be a winner and a loser when it came to natural resource management on public lands. For these people, development of natural resources resulted in an economic win, while conservation resulted in an economic loss.

Management of public lands and decisions about who should benefit from them has also been shaped by a dichotomy in the form of a rural/urban divide.[99] Painting with a very broad brush, we can say that natural resource conservation has been supported by urban residents, while development and extraction of natural resources has been supported by rural residents. This divide has contributed to a perception that urban elites are interfering in the livelihoods of rural residents. Taken a step further, it has been viewed as the willful intention of urban elites to deny rural communities their right to fulfill their economic destiny and a way of forcing poverty upon them.

It is from these perceptions that the Sagebrush Rebellion of the late 1970s and early 1980s was born, which saw pockets of western resentment boil over, along with demands that the federal government relinquish control of federal public lands and place those lands and their management in the hands of the western states. Behind these calls was a distrust of federal policies—a sense that public lands were being mismanaged since the natural resources contained within them were not being exploited to the greatest possible extent. An attendant belief was that the western states could better manage public lands by opening them up for greater exploitation and for the economic windfall that would presumably follow.[100] It is worth noting that during this period, there was little to no consideration by these groups of the considerable investment and expertise required to manage public lands or of the potential for creating boom-bust cycles that would impoverish rural residents rather than set them free from economic uncertainty.

It is against this socially and culturally complex backdrop of public land management that the reintroduction of gray wolves was viewed in the Rocky Mountains, and my home state of Wyoming was no exception. Although I was still quite young, I distinctly remember the heated debates that took place at kitchen tables and in public meetings about the reintroduction efforts. I remember my second stepfather recalling how his grandfather had helped purge wolves from the countryside and declaring that he would be damned if he'd allow them to come back to terrorize stockmen. At almost no point did I hear anyone proclaim the benefits associated with the reintroduction of wolves to Yellowstone National Park or the larger ecosystem; instead, thinly veiled or open threats of violence were commonly voiced by the adults that surrounded me. These included not only the "shoot, shovel, and shut up" exclamations that became so common but also threats of violence against people who supported wolf reintroduction and against those charged with management of the species and its recovery.

The concerted and government-supported extermination of wolves throughout the country was the reason my grandfather had chuckled the night Brandon and I asked if it was wolves we heard in the darkness outside the cabin. Little did I know that when Brandon and I asked that question, efforts were already afoot to return wolves to the landscape. It wouldn't be until I attended graduate school that I would understand the role wolves play in an ecosystem and would develop my own understanding of wolf conservation beyond the vitriolic debate and open hostility to the species I encountered as a child during the reintroduction era.

SUCCESS & CONTROVERSY

Fifteen years after wolves were reintroduced to Yellowstone National Park, the wolf population had successfully rebounded. The wolves released into Yellowstone were designated an experimental, nonessential population, a definition placed within the Endangered Species Act after it was amended in 1982. The designation provided the U.S. Fish and Wildlife Service a high degree of flexibility when it came to managing the released wolves and their offspring. Importantly, it allowed for "take"—in other words, the killing of individuals and packs—as necessary to protect livestock.

One of the critical components of the reintroduction plan was the explicit understanding that problem wolves that preyed on livestock would be lethally removed. In the Greater Yellowstone Ecosystem and the Bighorn Basin, ranching is conducted on public lands as well as on private ones. Although the livestock industry was dead set against supporting the reintroduction, the guarantee that problem wolves could be killed, coupled with the establishment of a reimbursement fund by a nonprofit conservation organization that supported wolf reintroduction, mitigated some of the angst within the ranching community.

The nonessential, experimental designation of the released wolves and their descendants provided the necessary flexibility to provide legitimacy to the restoration effort. The result was a wolf population that expanded into the available habitat within Yellowstone National Park, and then expanded further into the national forests surrounding the park, which are recognized as the Greater Yellowstone Ecosystem. The successful reintroduction of wolves into the northern Rocky Mountains would be validated in 2008 by a declaration from the Fish and Wildlife Service that it would pursue removal of the gray wolf from the Endangered Species list in the reintroduction states, with the exception of Wyoming.

The announcement of wolf recovery was met with approval by those who believed wolf numbers were already too high and that the states, rather than the federal government, should be in charge of wolf management. Echoes of the Sagebrush Rebellion could be heard behind many of these arguments. Others, particularly nonprofit organizations, both local and national in scale, condemned the announcement. The result would be another bitter battle between supporters of wolf conservation and their opponents. The battle over removing the wolf from the Endangered Species list would largely be played out in courthouses, as both sides used the courts to pursue the enactment of their beliefs through litigation.

The attempt to delist the gray wolf in Wyoming has followed a particularly torturous path through the halls of Congress and the courts.[101] The gray wolf was first delisted in 2012 in Wyoming, but in 2014 a lower court ruling removed the wolves from state management and returned them to the protections of the Endangered Species Act. This ruling was reversed on March 3, 2017, by the U.S. Court of Appeals for the District of Columbia, which again removed Wyoming's wolf population from under the Endangered Species Act and again allowed the state to manage wolves within its borders. The state, as it did when wolves were first delisted in 2012, plans to allow wolves to be shot on sight throughout most of the state, while also establishing a seasonal hunt in the northwest corner of Wyoming, largely in the national forest lands that border Yellowstone National Park and Grand Teton National Park.

After coming home from overseas, I had taken to returning home to hunt every fall in order to reconnect with friends and family; also, having some game meat in the freezer was a benefit for a cash-strapped graduate student. On one of these trips, as two friends and I drove up a muddy and slick mountain road in the predawn darkness to reach our elk-hunting area outside Cody, Wyoming, an offhand comment about the impact of wolves on elk herds quickly ignited a heated discussion over the consequences of wolf reintroduction and whether or not it should have been undertaken in the first place. As we ascended the mountain in the dark, we decided that the topic of wolves would be banned from our conversation, since we were too far apart in our beliefs to discuss the topic without tempers flaring.

The effect of wolves on populations of deer, elk, moose, and other hunter-pursued game species has become a centerpiece of the argument for state control of wolf management. Our disagreement in the truck that morning began with just such a discussion. But one thing appears clear, at least to me: wolves have an ecological role to play within their native ecosystems and therefore deserve to be part of the landscape. While some, including some wolf biologists, see this as nothing more than a scientific veneer to a value-based admonition, I find myself returning to Aldo Leopold and his insightful understanding of the natural world. In his essay "The Land Ethic," he states: "A thing is right when it tends to preserve the integrity, stability, and beauty of the biotic community. It is wrong when it tends otherwise."[102] Contained in this wonderfully elegant statement is an understanding of the amazing complexity that comprises functional ecosystems. Additionally, Leopold's land ethic recognizes the need to maintain, as closely as possible, each individual piece of an ecosystem, as our own ignorance of the complexities of the natural world will prevent us from understanding the true impacts associated with removing individual components of the system. In short, maintaining the structural integrity of an ecosystem is the ultimate ecological insurance policy.

Acknowledging our own ignorance is an important element of conservation, which is why it is crucial to maintain all the pieces of an ecosystem and, by extension, protect and recover species that are imperiled with extinction. Even though our knowledge of individual species and ecosystems continues to increase, the complexity of ecosystems and their individual components prevents us from knowing with any certainty the cascading consequences of the loss of any species, especially in the long term. We may be able to identify the first-order impacts to predators, prey, or competitors, but the challenge increases exponentially when we try to ascertain second- and third-order effects that ripple throughout food webs and potentially influence physical and biogeochemical processes within an ecosystem. For this reason alone, it is important to maintain our native wolf populations, despite the cultural prejudices against the species.

The wolf sits atop the food chain in the ecosystems it inhabits throughout the world. In many ecosystems, it shares this top rung of the ladder with other apex predators such as the grizzly bear, the black bear, and, in the Rocky Mountains, the mountain lion. As a generalist predator, the gray wolf preys on a wide range of species, from the minute field mouse to the massive bison. In the modern era, competition with humans, particularly hunters in pursuit of ungulates in the form of deer, elk and moose, has developed into a new point of conflict for wolf management. While the gray wolf is not exclusively carnivorous, the hoofed prey that hunters prefer to pursue does serve as the basis of the wolf diet in North America, particularly during winter.[103] Even though the numbers of hunters in the United States has been trending downward over the last few decades, the perceived competition with wolves for deer, elk, and moose continues to fuel resistance to wolf reintroduction and federal wolf management.

While wolves undoubtedly have a direct impact on populations of native hoofed prey species, a longer-term perspective is necessary when discussing the effect wolves have on ungulate populations, and Yellowstone National Park and the larger Greater Yellowstone Ecosystem can serve as a perfect example. When wolves were first reintroduced to Yellowstone National Park and the larger Greater Yellowstone, many supporters of reintroduction believed the wolves could help balance ecological impacts stemming from elk herds that were considered to be on the verge of surpassing (or possibly already had surpassed) the carrying capacity of their habitat. Popular and scientific publications during this period decried the destruction to riparian vegetation and aspen stands caused by large elk herds in Yellowstone, in particular.[104] The reintroduction of wolves was expected to help reduce these herds, relieving some of the pressure on riparian vegetation and aspen stands, which would then create additional impacts throughout the food web.

Subsequent research in Yellowstone National Park and elsewhere demonstrated that the reintroduction of gray wolves did, in fact, produce positive ecological effects within these ecosystems. In some cases, streamside riparian vegetation, including the willows that are so critically important to beavers, moose, and a variety of birds that use riparian shrubs, were allowed to recover, benefitting the larger ecosystem, including the aquatic environment.[105] The reduction in overbrowsing by elk allowed beavers, who compete with elk for riparian forage, to recolonize areas long since abandoned. As discussed in the previous chapter, these beavers can produce a number of positive effects, including the recharging of the water table and the reestablishment of wetlands that provide habitat for a variety of species—aquatic, terrestrial, and avian alike.[106] While reintroduction of a native predator is not necessarily a panacea for all ecosystem ills, there are clearly positive benefits from maintaining the basic ecological structure of an ecosystem.

While both willow stands and beaver populations recovered in some watersheds that saw reduced pressure from excessive browsing by elk herds, not all areas were as fortunate. In some watersheds that had been abandoned by beavers and where the riparian willows had been extensively overbrowsed, willows faltered and failed to take hold, which in turn, prevented beavers from returning. Without the return of beavers, willows stayed stunted, streams remained incised rather than gathering behind a dam, and the water table stayed too low to promote increased willow growth that would entice the beavers, all of which resulted in a positive feedback loop to the detriment of the ecosystem.[107] In situations such as this, it takes more than the reestablishment of a top-tier predator to return an ecosystem to its original condition and function.

Management of wolves, whether it be their eradication from the landscape, reintroduction, or ongoing management, will continue to be a point of conflict in the Rocky Mountains. This conflict hardly skipped a beat after the U.S. Fish and Wildlife Service declared the species recovered and began the process of delisting the gray wolf and turning over management to the states.

Lawsuit upon lawsuit pushed management authority back and forth between the federal and state governments.

A key component of wolf management in the Rocky Mountains is harvest of the species. Many wolf biologists have recognized that in order for wolves and humans to occupy the same ecosystems, limited lethal removal will be a necessity.[108] I tend to agree with this sentiment. If we step back and look at the extent to which ecosystems, even ones that are considered intact and largely undeveloped, are managed for the benefit of human communities—whether that benefit be water, wildlife, agriculture, energy extraction, or pollutions sinks—we must acknowledge that maintaining gray wolf population levels in a way that allows for their continued acceptance on the landscape will require harvest. It is also likely that, in order to maintain the ecological role of gray wolves in the Greater Yellowstone Ecosystem, lethal removal will be required, just as harvest is required for ungulates in this seemingly wild, but in reality quite heavily managed, ecosystem.

The predation of wolves on livestock is one of the historical causes of hatred for the wolf, a hatred that has pursued it across continents. It is a social injustice to force a single group of citizens—in this instance, the ranching community—to bear the weight of wolf recovery in the Rocky Mountains. Providing mechanisms that allow ranchers to cope with the loss of livestock is imperative to maintaining their engagement, grudging as it may be, in maintaining wolves in the Rocky Mountains. Of course, the killing of problem wolves is only one tool, along with preventive measures and mechanisms to recompense ranchers for the loss of livestock and the financial burden that accompanies wolf predation on livestock.

Although there is much work to be done, I believe that with reasonable compromise and further effort, the gray wolf that is native to the northern Rocky Mountains may once again become a permanent part of this landscape. And I hope that if my children ever have the opportunity to ask me one warm summer evening, as we gather around the family dining table at Rubyat, if the howls they hear in the darkness are wolves, I will be able to answer, "Yes."

CHAPTER 12

It Takes an Ecosystem

THE FOREST SERVICE ROAD TO the cabin had been closed to all but administrative traffic after wildfire swept over the mountain. Now, two years after the fire, the road was finally reopened for public travel. From behind the car windshield, I could see that the lodgepole pine forest that I had known my whole life had been obliterated. The rush of the flames had left little behind in its wake. Tightly packed lodgepole pine forest on both sides of the road had been replaced with an ashen wasteland. Magnificent hillsides had been denuded and were painfully eroding, even as plants sought to take hold on their barren surfaces. Entire stands of pines were now reduced to lonesome burnt matchsticks surrounded by scorched earth and ash. This was the tortured rebirth of an ecosystem.

Landmarks had disappeared in the transformed landscape. Even the road I once knew by heart followed a slightly different course in this now unfamiliar landscape. I turned the car around twice, trying to find the spot where the road to the cabin had branched from the main Forest Service road. I finally gave up and put the car in park in a safe spot near where I thought the road to the cabin had been. Unable to find any semblance of a familiar landmark in this post-fire desolation, I decided to walk to the stream. The smell of smoke was still pervasive, even this long after the fire, and every step sent up a puff of powdery ash. The stream flowed clean and clear as always, but below the surface the multihued cobblestones were smothered in a gray blanket of ash and mud. As I walked downstream, the rock island came into view as a mud-crusted shade of its former self. Where once the island had been hidden behind a verdant curtain, it now stood naked for all to see. Once I found the rock island, I was able to quickly orient myself in this forlorn former forest.

The clearing where the cabin had stood for over one hundred years had been annihilated. Every log of the cabin had been consumed, as had nearly every lodgepole pine that once surrounded it. A shiver went through me as I spied a large boulder partially obscured by ash and tufts of newly regenerated grass. As I approached the boulder, my shoes stirred ash where once there had been only grass. Large river stones began to materialize within the ash, as I searched for any relic of the cabin. What I discovered were the remnants of the chimney and the foundational boulder upon which it had been built. The only remains of my family's legacy were those that could not be burned: displaced river stones and a burned-over boulder on a hilltop.

This apocalyptic scene is from a nightmare I had during my first solo trip to the cabin as a young man in college. I have no doubt that the nightmare was spawned by my pervasive fear of sparking a wildfire after coaxing forth a small fire in the cabin's river-rock fireplace the first night of my stay. The horror of that dream has stayed with me throughout the years.

FIRE & FLOOD

Wildfire, flood, hurricane, earthquake, tsunami: disaster! Undoubtedly when the forces of nature destroy human communities and lives, these are indeed disasters. But there are a great many times when what might otherwise be viewed as a disaster is, in fact, a boon to an ecosystem. In ecology we recognize these events as disturbances. Ecological research throughout the world has determined that, for a great many ecosystems, disturbance is a means of restoring ecosystem health and function.[109] This is true of the montane Wyoming landscape of my home-waters.

Every spring, anglers anxiously await warmer weather while at the same time keeping watch for reports that the spring thaw has begun to release its hold on the high slopes of the Rocky Mountains. Whether by official report, by secondhand information from other anglers, or by visiting a favorite stream or river looking for the requisite high waters churning with sediment and debris, we anglers are all familiar with the seasonal spring runoff. We intuitively know that this seasonal flooding is part of a normal ecosystem rhythm. Anglers recognize seasonal flooding as an important component of the health of a river and of the adjacent floodplains that receive the inundation of water and materials during the flood, even in years when the flooding is particularly severe.

Over time, and for a variety of reasons, society has lost sight of the positive benefits associated with seasonal floods. One of the main reasons for this is that we can no longer see seasonal flooding that inundates floodplains and the riparian portions of an ecosystem as a benefit to the ecosystem; we have internally disconnected the waters that flow past us as tied to the lands that surround the river basin. This is most evident in areas where we have built our homes and economies on floodplains.

Resulting damage from seasonal floods to communities within a floodplain are viewed first and foremost as disasters, and, if accompanied by the loss of life and livelihood, as tragedies. And, in these circumstances, undoubtedly they are. But it is because we have lost our recognition of the role of flooding in the ecosystem that we have allowed ourselves to attempt to appropriate the lands of the floodplain for homes and industry. We have made massive industrial-scale investments in maintaining our hold on the floodplains, but too often have discovered that our best attempts at taming rivers are all too easily thwarted by the hand of nature. As anglers, we recognize the beneficial role of seasonal flooding on our favorite stream, but we often fail to recognize that the same dynamic holds true throughout rivers and floodplains across the country. The result is that we see disaster, rather than disturbance, when flooding takes place. The same dynamic holds true for the forested mountains of Wyoming and the streams and rivers that are the product of runoff from seasonal snowpack and rains.

Two important dynamics have interacted to influence our view of forest disturbance as disaster rather than as a healthy ecosystem function: natural resource policy and short-term baselines. The first dynamic is the historical legacy of fire policy in our forested mountain landscapes. Following the establishment of the forest reserves of the United States and of the Forest Service, the utilitarian view of Gifford Pinchot, America's first chief forester, was that forests were to be managed as a crop. This utilitarian approach viewed fire (and any other disturbance that precluded the use of timber for harvest and human use) as detrimental to overall forest health, resulting in a policy that all fires must be suppressed. It was an effective policy and a credit to the Forest Service, as well as to the other federal and state agencies that upheld this policy, that they met with a great deal of success. From a natural resource management and industry standpoint, the fire suppression policy was the correct policy prescription, since it maintained forests to be harvested. What wasn't readily obvious was that the policy was disrupting the role fire had played in forest ecosystems throughout the country. Ultimately, in many instances, the policy set the stage for catastrophic wildfires, which would most likely have been either intense and small in scale or large and of relatively low intensity had the natural fire regime been maintained.[110]

The second dynamic that has led us to this conundrum confounds the first. We tend to view change in the world through the lens of a human life span, and we develop many of our natural resource policies to reflect this bias. This way of thinking makes it very difficult for contemporary natural resource managers to convince the general public that a fire should be allowed to rage, even if it will ultimately be beneficial to the ecosystem. In many cases, the time it will take for an ecosystem to recover will exceed the life span of those watching the result of the unfurling fire—and quite possibly it will exceed their children's life spans as well. In some ecosystems, it will take multiple human generations to see the long-term benefit of wildfire on ecosystem health.

I was eight years old the morning I ran outside to play in the yard in Thermopolis, Wyoming, and found the light-green fiberglass picnic table covered in a fine gray ash. I had known that Yellowstone National Park was burning ferociously; it had been the dominant topic of conversation among the adults. But even after someone explained to me that the ash had been carried by the wind from the massive fires to the northwest, I remained perplexed by the ash on our table. I also distinctly remember the negative comments that followed the posting of "Blackstone National Park" on the sign of Granny's Ice-Cream Shoppe in town. The sign reflected the thoughts of many in the gateway communities of Yellowstone that the fires burning in the park would produce disastrous consequences, but the public display of that sentiment was, for reasons I couldn't fathom at eight years old, considered unacceptable.

My parents and the other adults around me believed the fires could spell the end of Yellowstone National Park. The "Blackstone" sign publicly voiced a private angst roiling the communities. Even though natural resource managers and scientists attempted to convince the general public that the ecological health of the forests would be maintained and even improved as a result of the fires, most people in the adjacent communities were skeptical and believed the fires would negatively affect the economies of their towns and, by extension, themselves.

The gateway communities that surround the entrances to Yellowstone National Park have developed robust tourism and recreation industries that rely in part on access to the park. A not insignificant portion of that industry is the sport fishing industry. Understandably, the view of those with economic skin in the game was that the fires would result in a potential loss of livelihood, whether that was as a fishing guide or as a waiter at a restaurant. While in circumstances such as these, it is understandable that people will worry about negative economic effects, we still need to question whether these legitimate concerns should be allowed to result in policies with long-term negative ecological consequences.

CREATIVE DESTRUCTION

Viewing ecosystems through a lens of short-term economic stability is what has often led to the catastrophic outcomes that we currently see in our forested ecosystems. Managing forests for short-term economic gain has resulted in considerable economic loss, as well as large-scale ecological devastation. A key source of this disconnect stems from viewing forest ecosystems within the time span of human life. Many of the processes of ecosystems, including the return time of wildfire, are considerably longer than that of a single human life span and, depending on the type of forest, may be as long as several hundred years.[111] Our inability to recognize and appreciate the long-term dynamics of the forest ecosystems (which are, of course, the uplands to our favorite streams, rivers, ponds, and lakes) prevents the development and implementation of natural resource policy that recognizes disturbance as a vital component of the ecosystem rather than a destructive force to be minimized.

We are currently experiencing the intersection of numerous disturbances within our forested ecosystems that have the potential to negatively affect both upland and aquatic environments. Even as we are still feeling the effects of our historical fire policy throughout large swaths of the western United States, we are also, in many ranges, confronting the impacts of a historic mountain pine beetle outbreak and the impacts of drought—and all these challenges are being exacerbated by the influences of climate change.[112]

The mountain pine beetle epidemic has left numerous mountainsides and valleys throughout the Rockies covered in red swaths of standing dead evergreens. Although scientific research hasn't been conclusive, the evidence available so far points to an increased fire danger in these swaths of dead trees, at least for a while.[113] The sight of massive beetle-killed stands of trees has produced rhetoric similar to the rhetoric surrounding episodes of catastrophic fires, with natural resource managers blamed for not allowing the more extensive harvesting that some seem to view as the panacea for all ecosystem ills. Economic calamity is predicted if radical efforts are not undertaken to remove all the standing dead timber. But, as with fires, before reacting, we should step back and look at the impacts of the mountain pine beetle at the ecosystem level.

The mountain pine beetle is an insect endemic to ecosystems throughout the Rocky Mountains (along with other beetles, including the spruce beetle and *Ips* beetle).[114] Beetle infestation is part of the disturbance cycle for these forested ecosystems. Although evidence is beginning to amass that climate change, mountain pine beetles, an altered fire regime, drought, and forest disease are all interacting to produce more widespread impacts than have been previously documented,[115] we must resist knee-jerk reactions to these disturbances. Mountain pine beetles play a significant role in the infestation-fire-regeneration cycle, particularly for lodgepole pine forests, such as those that surround my family cabin and are common across the Bighorn Mountains and throughout the Rockies.[116]

The contemporary impacts of ecosystem disturbance that affect our mountain forests and waters are widespread and obvious to the human eye, but we should not allow them to be used as an excuse to implement rash and ecologically detrimental natural resource policies. There can be little doubt that large-scale wildfire and mountain pine beetle infestations can have a negative impact, both independently and synergistically, on our favorite waters and their populations of trout, whether native or wild. Nevertheless, policies must be crafted, with input from natural resource managers as well as the local general public, that recognize there will be changes to the landscape following these disturbances. Only by embracing these changes can we develop natural resource policies that focus on long-term ecosystem health for both the upland and aquatic habitats following disturbance, one that recognizes that, on a long enough timeline, those areas currently untouched by disturbance will eventually feel its impacts.

Native trout, such as the Yellowstone and westslope cutthroat trout, have evolved in a landscape that periodically received intense wildfires. Native trout of the Rocky Mountains have evolved to possess the traits necessary to allow them to either survive or recolonize streams following a significant burn.[117] The trout populations survived the famous Yellowstone fires of 1988 just fine.[118] But this assumes that the fire in question is within the historical parameters of the ecosystem and that the resilience of the ecosystem is capable of withstanding the conflagration, which, in the contemporary world, can no longer be assumed. So although native trout in fire-prone ecosystems likely possesses the evolutionary traits for survival, whether those traits allow native trout to withstand the impacts from a historically unprecedented fire is certainly open to question.

While conducting research for my doctoral dissertation, I had the good fortune to live in the Flathead Valley of northwest Montana and fish the three forks of the Flathead River. My favorite fishing spots were found along the dirt road that often parallels the North Fork of the Flathead, as it flows south from the Canadian border and serves as the western boundary of Glacier National Park. The ecological reminders of past wildfires could be spotted from numerous vantage points along the river. As I worked my way up the river, alternating between casting to deep pools and terrific riffles in search of native westslope cutthroat trout, I would often take a moment to note the small stands of bone-white snags jutting from regenerating forests.

Each snag told a story of the intersection of past management practices and ecological realities. It is likely that many of the snags that stood as distant sentinels told the story of the enormous fires of 1910, an episode of landscape-wide catastrophic fires that helped set the stage for the policy of fire suppression. The sweeping conflagration of 1910 saw President Taft order the army to assist the Forest Service and the threatened communities fight the widespread fires. The inferno would help shape the Forest Service and its view of how to treat fire for generations.[119] Just as the fires and mountain pine beetle outbreak of the twenty-first century have left a mark on the landscape, as well as on the psyche of natural resource managers and the public, so did the fires of 1910. But as I watched my dry fly skate across the glassy waters of the North Fork, as they reflected the towering mountains, I appreciated that the fires also had contributed to the regeneration and long-term health of the ecosystem.

Just out the back door of the cabin, no more than ten paces away, arrow-straight evergreens sway harmoniously in the gentle mountain breeze. These giants are mature lodgepole pines, and you must crane your neck looking up at them before you see a single branch on their trunks, as most shed their lower limbs as they grow, leaving branches concentrated from the middle of their trunk to the top.

The lodgepole pines that surround the cabin and dominate the mid-elevations of much of the Bighorn Mountains depend on fire for their life cycle and ecological health. Lodgepoles grow densely packed after rising from the soil following a conflagration. Heat from the fire over the soil melts the waxy cover over the cones, allowing the seeds to germinate. At the same time, wildfire opens the evergreen canopy to allow sunlight to reach the ground, provides a pulse of nourishment from the ash that settles over the recently burned area, and removes the threat of competition with older established trees within the burn footprint. Densely packed saplings spring forth from the soil and compete with one another for dominance. While the best competitors among the fresh recruits will outcompete many of their neighbors, the regenerating stand will continue to be tightly packed with juvenile trees well into maturation, setting the stage for an intense wildfire to again rage through the stand, killing the mature trees and setting the ecological stage for the next crop of lodgepoles to replace them.[120]

The species is built for what is considered by humans to be catastrophic wildfire. Developing policies that embrace the need for disturbances to maintain the health of the ecosystem is critical to ensuring long-term ecosystem health. For natural resource managers, as well as many scientists, one of the primary obstacles to embracing disturbance is the view that ecosystems are systems that tend toward equilibrium rather than systems that are intrinsically dynamic and ever changing. The idea that forests move along a linear trajectory and tend toward equilibrium is well established in ecological thought and theory. Within this view of ecosystem dynamics, disturbance is an exogenous force that pushes the ecosystem from its equilibrium, and then a distinct amount of time is required for the ecosystem to return to its equilibrium.[121] Why is this important? The answer lies in the view of the role of disturbance within an ecosystem. If we recognize that, in many ecosystems (of which the lodgepole pine forest is an excellent example), disturbance is a critical component of ecosystem function rather than an outside force, natural resource managers can develop policies and strategies to allow disturbance to take place in a way that maintains ecosystem health—with the understanding, of course, that there will be limitations to the physical areas of landscapes where such a policy can be adequately implemented.

Just as there are a great deal of ecological benefits to allowing disturbances in an ecosystem to play their appropriate role, there are also times when it is appropriate to protect natural resources from disturbance. Fire may be part of an ecosystem's natural disturbance regime, but allowing the debris and sediment flow that follows a high-intensity fire in a watershed that holds one of the last remaining pure populations of threatened greenback cutthroat trout constitutes an unacceptable risk. In circumstances such as this, policy goals need to align with the ecological realities of the ecosystem in question.

There are a great many opportunities throughout the Rocky Mountains and beyond to support the return of disturbance to ecosystems. In the continental United States, it is difficult to find an ecosystem, even one dominated by wilderness, that is not affected by human activities. Many of these ecosystems, particularly those that reside largely or entirely within public lands, can and will benefit from natural resource policies that accept change as a fundamental function of an ecosystem and that recognize that natural disturbance is the most powerful catalyst for ecosystem change. Maintaining the role of disturbance in an ecosystem is a powerful insurance policy in ensuring that the ecosystems that contain our favorite waters maintain their health and ecological integrity. The concept of ecosystem resilience embraces the role of disturbance within an ecosystem and serves as a means for anglers and conservationists to engage natural resource policymakers on the long-term health of ecosystems, as well as the need to maintain the ecosystem's natural disturbance regime.

ECOLOGICAL RESILIENCE

Not unlike salmon in the Pacific Northwest, native trout in the Rocky Mountains require more than a healthy aquatic environment in which to survive; they need healthy forests to support a healthy watershed. The ability of Rocky Mountain forests to sustain the entirety of their functions and processes requires ecological resilience. In this case, *resilience* means specifically the ability of an ecosystem to absorb the shock of disturbance and continue to function.[122] When resilience is viewed through this lens, we implicitly accept the idea that disturbances can overwhelm the capacity of the ecosystem, often with a detrimental outcome to both the ecosystem and the communities that rely on the goods and services supplied by it. A catastrophic fire that decimates entire watersheds as the result of decades of fire suppression is a good example. Not only is the forest itself lost, the waters themselves are affected in the near term by the flow of sediment and debris. In the mid-to-long term, snowpack that was released slowly over the course of the spring and summer from beneath the shaded mountainsides is instead flushed off the mountain in rapid fashion, again carrying with it debris and sediment that choke the waters below. Thus we can see the importance of maintaining resilience in our forested ecosystems. Managing ecosystems for resilience will not preclude disturbance such as wildfire but will increase the likelihood that the intensity, scope, and scale of disturbances and their impacts are such that ecosystems are more likely to be left intact following a disturbance.

The concept of ecosystem resilience was originally developed by C. S. Holling in 1973 and was impressively expanded on in 1986 (and many more times thereafter).[123] Since Holling's introduction of the idea of ecological resilience, scientists have taken up the concept and applied it to ecosystems throughout the globe, expanding it to include the role that humans play in an ecosystem.[124] Of course, not all stresses that are placed on ecosystems result from natural disturbance regimes; many are the result of direct or indirect human activities (e.g., pollution, habitat fragmentation, and biodiversity loss).

In his early work conceptualizing ecosystem resilience, Holling introduced a four-part diagram that looked like a figure eight laying on its side, or, more directly, the infinity symbol. The symbol was drawn and labeled as an ecosystem's adaptive cycle. This depiction included exploitation, conservation, creative destruction (i.e., disturbance, and labeled in later works as "release"), and renewal. It is the third portion of the cycle that we have been discussing in detail—creative destruction, which in our case takes the form of disturbance. The adaptive cycle explicitly recognizes two important things: 1) that disturbance is a natural part of many ecosystems and leads to ecosystem renewal, as long as disturbance doesn't overwhelm an ecosystem's resilience; and 2) that change is always present in the natural world.

When the cumulative impacts of human activities place overwhelming stress on ecosystems, they eventually lose their resilience and can no longer withstand the disturbances that they have historically been capable of handling. The danger in allowing ecosystem resilience to be overwhelmed is that we may ultimately lose that which we love so much—our mountain forests and our favorite waters, as well as our chosen sport on those waters.

CHAPTER 13

The Trout & the Bear

It's not often that a guided fishing trip results in a wholesale shift in coldwater fishery management. In some ways, though, this is precisely what happened on July 30, 1994, after a guide who had taken a client fishing on Yellowstone Lake approached a ranger in Yellowstone National Park with a nineteen-inch lake trout his client had caught.[125] Shock at the catch—and at what the ramifications were for Yellowstone Lake and its native cutthroat trout—was instant and overwhelming.

Prior to the discovery of the lake trout, Yellowstone Lake had been considered the most significant stronghold for Yellowstone cutthroat trout.[126] The lake and its tributaries maintained a thriving YCT population, even though the species had lost ground throughout its historical habitat as a result of habitat loss, competition with non-native species, and hybridization with rainbow trout and other subspecies of cutthroat trout. During the early era of the park, it was believed that Yellowstone Lake and its native cutthroat trout were a boundless cornucopia; in fact, it was commonplace for tourists to catch tremendous amounts of fish, pose for a picture with their bounty, and then pitch the fish in the trash.

Fishery biologists and park managers realized immediately what the discovery of lake trout in Yellowstone Lake meant: the potential loss of what had been described as the greatest remaining Yellowstone cutthroat trout stronghold in the world. Bob Barbee, the Yellowstone superintendent, called it "an appalling act of environmental vandalism."[127] John Varley, the director of the Yellowstone Center for Resources recalled that he "felt physically ill."[128]

The Yellowstone Cutthroat Trout

The National Park Service reacted quickly, convening a workshop in February 1995 to determine what threat lake trout posed to the Yellowstone Lake ecosystem and its fisheries and to provide guidance on management actions to mitigate the impacts of the lake trout.[129] Participants in the workshop acknowledged that it was unlikely that lake trout could ever be eradicated from Yellowstone Lake and identified suppression of the lake trout population as the action most likely to be effective in salvaging at least a semblance of the lake's YCT population. The report concluded that with aggressive suppression of lake trout, the YCT population might decline by only 30 percent, and that without aggressive management, 70 percent of the YCT population would likely be lost within the next one hundred years.[130] Unfortunately, these estimates would prove to be far too rosy, as Yellowstone Lake, its tributaries, and its cutthroat trout population would be assaulted by a number of additional factors that would push the native trout toward local extinction.

One of the factors was the discovery of whirling disease in Yellowstone waters, which placed additional stress on the besieged Yellowstone cutthroat trout population. Whirling disease, so called because the infecting parasite causes deformities in the cartilage along the skeleton, which causes the infected fish to swim in circles, was first discovered in tributaries to Yellowstone Lake in 1998. Clear Creek, a major spawning tributary for the Yellowstone cutthroat trout of Yellowstone Lake, was the hardest hit and saw a precipitous drop in the number of spring spawners using the creek—from more than 54,000 in 1988[131] to a discouraging 489 in 2006, the lowest number recorded since monitoring began in 1945.[132] Pelican Creek, the second largest tributary to Yellowstone Lake, was described as "essentially lost" in 2004, even though in 1981 as many as 30,000 spawning cutthroat trout had been counted in the stream.[133] At Bridge Creek, only a single cutthroat trout returned to the tributary in 2004, a 99 percent decline since spawning counts were initiated in 1999.[134] Pelican Creek may be seeing a modest recovery and was reopened to fishing in 2011, after having been closed to help curtail the spread of whirling disease.[135]

An extended drought that lasted from 1998 to 2004 added additional misery to Yellowstone Lake's beleaguered cutthroat trout population. The drought was partially blamed for a reduction in peak flows, causing stream-flows late in the year to decline to such an extent that some tributary streams no long reached the lake. The drought has also been blamed for stranding cut-throat trout fry in disconnected side channels, preventing the juvenile trout from making their way to the lake.[136]

Given these numerous compounding stresses on Yellowstone Lake and its native cutthroat trout, the introduction of lake trout can be understood as highly significant for the Yellowstone cutthroat trout population and the larger ecosystem. Yellowstone cutthroat trout serve as a vital connection be-tween the aquatic and upland components of the Yellowstone Lake ecosystem. The consumption of Yellowstone cutthroat trout by predators, particularly, but not limited to, predation during spring spawning runs in the tributaries of the lake, moves nutrients from the lake to the riparian and terrestrial envi-ronments.[137] One of the greatest concerns of fisheries managers related to the introduction of lake trout to Yellowstone Lake is the ecological ripple effect lake trout would produce throughout the ecosystem. Lake trout do not utilize the various habitats of the lake and its tributaries in the same manner as cut-throat trout do, which managers recognized would prevent lake trout from occupying the same niche within the food web as Yellowstone cutthroat trout.

Lake trout spawn in the lake itself rather than running up the surround-ing tributaries to spawn as native cutthroat trout do, denying predators an op-portunity to consume large numbers of lake trout and disrupting the critical transfer of nutrients from the lake back to the upland environment. Even birds that typically prey on the YCT in Yellowstone Lake itself are often denied op-portunities to prey on the lake trout, since they tend to inhabit deeper waters for a significant portion of the year.

Increases in lake trout numbers also lead to a direct increase in preda-tion of Yellowstone cutthroat trout by the introduced non-native. A bioener-getics model predicted that the average lake trout would consume forty-one Yellowstone cutthroat trout per year, which in 1996 equated to fifteen metric tons or 14 percent of the total Yellowstone Lake cutthroat trout population.[138] The 1995 panel convened by the Park Service to address the issue of the illegal lake trout stocking and the population growth of the species recognized that the non-native invader would likely become a keystone predator, reshaping Yellowstone Lake's food web.[139] In 2010, research confirmed that the introduction of lake trout had, indeed, restructured the lake's food web.[140]

Some people initially believed that suppression of the lake trout population through netting and possibly other means, such as identifying spawning areas and then disrupting spawning, would prevent lake trout from destroying the Yellowstone cutthroat trout fishery. The unfortunate reality is that the lake trout invasion, coupled with the prolonged drought and the impacts of whirling disease, decimated the lake's cutthroat trout population. In 2005, fisheries biologists working in Yellowstone National Park noted that "the cutthroat trout population size of this system was once considered to be in the millions: however, current abundance indices suggest that only a fraction of that population exists today."[141]

Although lake trout were first confirmed in Yellowstone Lake in 1994, it was eventually determined that they had been in the lake since at least 1989[142] and that they had likely been introduced from Lewis Lake.[143] Lewis Lake was one of the nearly 40 percent of Yellowstone's waters that were fishless at the time of the park's establishment. Barren waters in the park were subject to the liberal stocking policies of the day and were the recipients of many introduced non-natives species.[144]

Following the recommendations set forth by the 1995 panel, Yellowstone National Park implemented a robust gillnetting regime, which continues to this day. A second panel was convened in 2008 to assess the efficacy and impact of the netting program and to determine where improvements could be made.[145] The panel found that despite the success and increasing efficiency of the lake trout gillnetting program, the lake trout population was continuing to increase as well and noted that "the program cannot succeed on the present budget." The panel did determine that YCT populations would be smaller and the lake trout population larger if the netting program had not been implemented. The panel concluded with a number of recommendations, many of which would require an increase in budget and personnel, a difficult proposition given that a report that had come out back in 2003 had concluded the netting operations were straining Yellowstone's fishery program at the expense of other priorities.[146] Nevertheless, the Park Service remains committed to the suppression of the lake trout population and the protection of the remaining Yellowstone Lake cutthroat trout. The park has moved forward with a novel recommendation from the second scientific review panel to hire commercial fishermen to assist in the lake trout suppression efforts by employing private-industry knowledge in commercial fishing and netting techniques. This effort was initiated in 2009 and continues through the time of this writing.[147]

THE GRIZZLY BEAR

The differing life cycles of Yellowstone cutthroat trout and lake trout ripple throughout both the aquatic and terrestrial environments of the Greater Yellowstone Ecosystem. Forty-two species in the Greater Yellowstone Ecosystem depend on the Yellowstone cutthroat trout to varying degrees.[148] A particularly visible case is the utilization of spawning YCT populations as a readily available source of food for Yellowstone's bears in the springtime.

Yellowstone's bear population has been a source of controversy for a lengthy portion of the park's history. In the 1880s, shortly after the creation of the park in 1872, park management condoned and supported the feeding of bears. Until 1940, the feeding of bears at garbage dumps and trash pits was, in fact, considered a tourist attraction. While the feeding continued, although out of sight of the general public, until 1970, it was discontinued after exposure to public, political, and scientific scrutiny.[149] It was believed, at the time, that bears would have to relearn fishing behavior after generations of receiving food from garbage dumps.[150] Just four years after discontinuation of bear feeding at dumps in the park, however, grizzlies were documented fishing along eleven spawning streams in Yellowstone. In 1974 and 1975, grizzlies were catching Yellowstone cutthroat trout on slightly less than 20 percent of the spawning streams of Yellowstone Lake.[151] By 1985, grizzly bears had dramatically expanded their use of Yellowstone cutthroat trout spawning runs as a food source and had increased their presence to 61 percent of spawning streams.

After the discovery of lake trout in Yellowstone Lake in 1994, researchers returned to the lake's spawning streams to again study the use of spawning cutthroat trout as a food source for the bears. They discovered that in the West Thumb portions of the lake and its tributaries, cutthroat trout numbers were in decline and, subsequently, so was grizzly activity in the area.[152] The species had been listed as "threatened" in 1975 under the Endangered Species Act, and the number of grizzlies fishing for Yellowstone cutthroat trout on the spawning tributaries of Yellowstone Lake would become central to the discussion of whether the grizzly population had recovered enough to be removed from the list.

In 2007, the U.S. Fish and Wildlife Service determined that the grizzly bear population in the Greater Yellowstone Ecosystem had reached its recovery milestones and therefore no longer required the protections of the Endangered Species Act. But a single species cannot be viewed independently of the ecosystem, and a number of environmental groups challenged the decision to delist the grizzly bear. In 2009, the groups took their challenge to court and found a sympathetic ear, particularly in their argument that numerous food sources for the grizzlies were under assault and therefore the grizzly population required continued protection.

TROUT, TREES, AND BEARS

The quandary over how to assess the Greater Yellowstone Ecosystem's grizzly bear population is tied to Yellowstone Lake and the condition of the lake's cutthroat trout population, although the debate is also complicated by other sources of food insecurity. Whitebark pines, which are a prime grizzly bear food source through the trees' nutritious seeds, are declining as a result of the historic mountain pine beetle outbreak discussed in the previous chapter. In addition to the mountain pine beetle, which is native to the Greater Yellowstone Ecosystem, a non-native disease, white pine blister rust, has placed additional stress on whitebark pines. As noted previously, the mountain pine beetle epidemic expanded into areas historically untouched by previous outbreaks, which include whitebark pine habitat. The whitebark pine has no defense against the mountain pine beetle infestation,[153] and as the infestation has decimated whitebark pine stands throughout the Greater Yellowstone

Ecosystem, the grizzly bear population has been deprived of a second highly nutritious, seasonally available food source.

Making a tough situation worse is that the beetle has been found to preferentially attack whitebark pine trees infected with blister rust.[154] Blister rust spreads from currants and gooseberries to infect white pines, which include the whitebark pine.[155] The disease causes cankers and branch dieback, resulting in reduced photosynthesis, reproductive failure, and ultimately death of the infected tree.[156] The combination of mountain pine beetle infestation and blister rust infection has been identified as the principal reason for the loss of whitebark pine,[157] with mortality estimates as high as 90 percent in some areas.[158]

Whitebark pines occupy a narrow habitat range in the Rocky Mountains, occurring from the upper subalpine zone to treeline.[159] The long-lived, slow-growing species typically begins producing cones and the nutritious seeds contained inside somewhere between twenty and thirty years of age but doesn't begin producing large crops of cones until around sixty to eighty years of age.[160] Whitebark pines have developed a trait known as masting that synchronizes large cone crops every three to five years.[161] This trait can be quite beneficial to grizzly bears, as it provides a ready food source in years when masting takes place.

Identified as both a keystone species and a foundational species within the ecosystems in which it is found, whitebark pine has coevolved with a bird called the Clark's nutcracker, resulting in a mutualistic relationship between the two species.[162] The Clark's nutcracker is quite remarkable in its ability to perpetuate the whitebark pine. The gray, black, and white bird can determine when seeds inside the cones of whitebark pine are ripe and therefore a ready source of food for the bird—and eventually other species.[163] It has been posited that a single Clark's nutcracker can harvest and cache a whopping ninety-eight thousand seeds in a single year![164] It's no wonder that the Clark's nutcracker has been credited with maintaining the distribution and abundance of the whitebark pine. Of course, the Clark's nutcracker is not the only species that harvests and caches the seeds of the whitebark pine. Red squirrels are efficient harvesters and cache large numbers of whitebark pine seeds, but it appears that few squirrel-cached seeds result in the germination and growth of new whitebark pines.[165] In contrast, Clark's nutcrackers seem to cache the seeds at the perfect soil depth that allows for successful germination and establishment of new whitebark pine seedlings.[166] Clark's nutcrackers also help regenerate whitebark pines in recently burned areas, helping to stabilize soil and allowing the area to regenerate from the disturbance.[167]

Whitebark pine seeds are a critical component of the grizzly bear diet, as the bears begin preparation for winter hibernation. Grizzly bears raid red squirrel middens that contain caches of the highly nutritious whitebark pine seeds, as the bears build up fat reserves for hibernation.[168] The trouble for grizzly bears is that the highly nutritious whitebark pine seeds, like the Yellowstone cutthroat trout, are under threat and declining.

Like the Yellowstone cutthroat trout, whitebark pine populations are threatened by a number of stresses. As a keystone species, whitebark pine influence ecosystem structure, function, and processes in the areas of the Greater Yellowstone Ecosystem where they are found.[169] The ability of the species to withstand the stress of the numerous assaults that are pummeling the species is of grave concern to scientists, natural resource managers, and conservationists, as well as to members of the general public concerned about ecological issues.

Aspects of past natural resource policies, coupled with a changing climate, are working in tandem to potentially drive the whitebark pine to extinction in the Greater Yellowstone Ecosystem. In many instances, whitebark pines facilitate the ability of other plants to take root and thrive by anchoring soil, collecting snow, and increasing soil moisture. And while they may facilitate the ability of other tree species to take root, they do not compete well with other tree species, largely because they are intolerant to shading from other nearby trees.[170] A century of fire suppression has allowed species that outcompete whitebark pine to persist in areas where they would likely have been swept away under a normal fire regime, which has undermined the ability of whitebark pine to flourish.[171] While there are a number of different fire regimes that have historically been associated with whitebark pine stands, fire suppression has allowed whitebark pines to be displaced by other tree species, including subalpine fir and Engelmann spruce. In many cases, it will take a high-intensity stand-replacement fire to return whitebark pine to their functional role in the ecosystem, but even then, the return will be successful only if there is a sufficient seed base available for the species to begin regeneration.

Decline of whitebark pine throughout its range prompted the Natural Resources Defense Council, an environmental nonprofit organization, to petition the U.S. Fish and Wildlife Service in 2008 to list the species as endangered throughout its entire range. Upon concluding a twelve-month status review of the best available scientific and commercial information, the U.S. Fish and Wildlife Service determined that the whitebark pine was deserving of listing and the protections offered under the Endangered Species Act, but a listing was precluded by the need to focus agency efforts and funding on higher-priority threatened and endangered species.[172]

Historical fire policies, the unprecedented mountain pine beetle epidemic, and the continuing spread of blister rust are only part of the story of the decline of the whitebark pine seed as a food source for grizzly bears. Climate change is reshaping and will continue to reshape many ecosystems, and the habitat of the whitebark pine is no exception. Models predicting the impacts of climate change on whitebark pine are extremely discouraging: a 70 percent decline beginning in 2030, with potentially a 97 percent decline in the current distribution of the species by the end of the century, has been predicted.[173] In addition to direct habitat loss, climate change may result in a shift of the Greater Yellowstone Ecosystem's fire regime to something unseen in either the historical record or human history.

From lake, to streambank, to grizzlies and trees, and to the wider ecosystem: we can observe how the impacts to a single species reverberate. The introduction of lake trout to Yellowstone Lake may, at first glance, appear as a grave threat primarily to the Yellowstone cutthroat trout, but as we've seen, the illegal stocking echoes throughout the entire ecosystem. The ripple effects throughout the food web demonstrate why our perspective on native trout conservation must be comprehensive enough to include the ecosystem in its scope as well.

Although it is not always immediately evident, our conservation efforts, even for what may seem like a small project, can create large-scale benefits. While the battle to suppress the lake trout population in Yellowstone Lake is an enormous endeavor, one that will continue into the foreseeable future, it could well have positive implications not only for the native Yellowstone cutthroat trout but for several other threatened species, as well as the health of the ecosystem as a whole.

CHAPTER 14

Returning to Rubyat

ANTHROPOCENE: WHAT A STRANGE WORD. Nevertheless, it sums up rather succinctly the idea that humans haven't just inherited the earth but have dominated it. We are living in the age of man. In the preceding chapters, we have journeyed along and into streams, through streamside riparian zones, and into the forests and the disturbances that rejuvenate them, while contemplating "how" to take an ecosystem-wide view of native trout conservation. But the "why" we should do so is encompassed in the jumble of letters that spell out *Anthropocene.*

Humans have reshaped every ecosystem we have come into contact with. We have created and destroyed coasts, razed forests, removed mountaintops, and stripped the oceans bare of not just individual species but entire food webs. We have left our mark on them all, and in doing so, have driven countless species to extinction. Woe be unto a species that stands in front of human progress: just ask the dodo, the passenger pigeon, and the yellowfin cutthroat trout.

So many species that share our world stand on the precipice of living on only in the pages of books that it boggles the mind and disquiets the soul. So rapid is the rate at which we have begun to remove other species from our world that we now rival the global decimation of an asteroid smashing into the surface of the earth: the result of humankind's domination of the blue planet has the force of a disastrous planetary event. The World Wildlife Fund has determined that just between the years 1970 and 2010, 52 percent of the wildlife on earth has perished![174] And so we've entered the sixth great extinction.

CAUTIOUS OPTIMISM

One result of all this destructive force is that the future survival of many of our remaining native species is clouded in uncertainty. We will only be able to stanch the bleeding from a thousand environmental cuts, and possibly even reverse the trend, if we are willing to think in wider ecological terms. In the case of native cutthroat trout, our view of the trout stream needs to be broadened to encompass the banks, species, uplands, and disturbances that surround that stream. Adopting an ecosystem-wide perspective transforms the way we think about conserving trout—all trout, but most importantly, native trout. Through this lens, we can discern that there are gains to be made throughout the environment once we open our minds to the connections nature has established, both obvious and obscure.

Even as we enter an age where human-induced climate change sweeps across the globe, it is very likely that trout will survive. Trout are an adaptable family that have not only sustained themselves during times of global disruption but, on an evolutionary timeline, have managed to reproduce, spread into new waters, colonize new habitats, and give rise to ever more species. Unfortunately, without assistance from humans—we are the species that, after all, placed native trout in their precarious predicament—it is highly unlikely that native trout will survive, especially once we take into account the effects that climate change will wreak on trout habitats. The addition of climate change to the numerous other stressors discussed throughout this book requires that we take thoughtful, strategic actions to conserve native trout, and it requires we do so in an environment where timelines are short and the repercussions for failure quite likely mean extinction.

The rapid rate of ecological change that is sweeping over the earth's biomes is likely to accelerate; the losers will be those species that can't adapt to such rapid changes in their environment. Luckily for trout, we have some practice in mitigating, to some extent, the impacts to coldwater habitats that climate change is likely to compound. Hatcheries, while historically the nemesis of native trout, will play an important role in maintaining native trout species, at least in the near term. However, hatcheries are only an interim step for native trout recovery. They will allow us to artificially maintain unique native trout populations, or in the worst of cases, the last remnants of an entire species. But this is only a narrow bridge to true recovery, one that can only take place after native trout have been reintroduced into their historical habitat to successfully reproduce for generations to come.

An Eye Toward the Future

One memorable day from my graduate school years: I was working in my advisor's natural resource policy lab at the University of New Hampshire. Graduate and undergraduate students filtered in and out throughout the day, as classes, food, and other diversions called. A handful of us were partaking in that exercise that all grad students excel in—procrastination—when a fellow grad student walked in and, without a word of introduction, proclaimed: "To be an ecologist today is to document the death of the world."

Our conversations came to a halt, as we waited for more words to follow. But there was only silence. The student had poured his frustration with studying ecology in today's world into those thirteen words; they fully conveyed his sense of defeat at cataloging daily environmental losses while trying to hold onto a glimmer of hope that he could contribute even a sliver of progress to the fight against global ecological decay.

Without connections to a community that holds your values, it's easy to suffocate under a wet blanket of heart-breaking news stories about human societies' continued degradation of our lands, waters, and wildlife. Retreating into social media to find digital kindred souls can be its own form of isolation. The human soul requires a personal connection that allows communion with other people who not only understand but empathize—which is exactly what my labmate needed from us that day. Fortunately, we were able to recognize that it was time to take a break from our work in the lab, and we reconvened at a bar near campus. Our conversation may not have been particularly inspiring, but it also wasn't the point, as we were able to draw strength from each other simply by nurturing the flame that had brought us together in the first place.

The global conservation community is deep, broad, and active. The members of that community may not seek you out, but I can guarantee that if you find them, they will not turn you away. During the revision process of this book, I had the opportunity to attend the first International Trout Congress in Bozeman, Montana, in the fall of 2016. The congress brought together lovers of trout from all walks of life and showcased trout biology, ecology, and conservation efforts from across the world, as well as beautiful works of art. Some of the most inspiring programs were those developed by educators to get kids not only out of the classroom and familiar with trout streams but also scientifically interested in the natural world around them. The congress was an important reminder that there is a large, if diffuse, community dedicated to conserving what we have for those who will inherit the world after our passing. Connecting with the conservation community is a significant part of the antidote for the fatigue that often comes with trying to preserve the lands, waters, and wildlife that we love. The paths that lead to the larger conservation community are truly boundless, and the door is always open.

The rock island of my youth has morphed over the years, reshaped by the hand of nature every spring, as rushing snowmelt waters plummet off the mountain. The island is now the leading edge of the stream channel, which turns and heads east instead of flowing around the one-time island to the bend in the stream that served as my childhood fishing limit. My daughter, at the age of three, "discovered" the rock island for herself, although to her the rock island is "the beach at the cabin!" She always says this phrase with gusto (and often accompanied with hand-clapping). The wonders of the cabin are at their peak for my daughter when, pail and shovel in hand, she joins me as we dig in the sand that has been deposited on the tail end of the rock island. Coming in a close second for her is watching from the porch swing as moose browse the willows surrounding the meadow.

Her discovery of the "beach at the cabin" took place when her baby brother was only eleven days old, during our first visit to the cabin as a newly expanded family. It was also during this time that I had the great pleasure of completing my final draft of this book while at home in the Bighorn Basin. I've been able to take many, many trips with my children to the cabin to visit the stream and the rock island (or, rather, "the beach at the cabin!")—and, I hope, in a few short years, to introduce them to fly fishing. The day is quickly approaching when my home-waters will become their home-waters.

I realize that the pressures that have led to the local extinction of Yellowstone cutthroat trout in Tensleep Creek below the cabin are unlikely to relent during my lifetime; nevertheless, I will continue to advocate and, when possible, put boots-on-the-ground to see them reintroduced to their native waters. This is far more than a generational struggle to conserve native trout and biodiversity—it is a generational gift, the opportunity to help preserve for my children the part of their birthright that is found in the public lands and waters of Wyoming.

If I had any illusions that calling for a realignment of generations-old fisheries policies in a way that favors native trout over wild trout was anything but a Herculean task, those illusions were quickly dispelled by watching, in the short time since I returned home, a native trout restoration project fail. In 2015 and 2016, as the Wyoming Game and Fish Department prepared a project to better secure and expand local populations of Yellowstone cutthroat trout, the local fisheries staff instituted a public outreach and information program. The department knew that there would be public resistance to removing brook trout from Eagle Creek, a tributary to the North Fork of the Shoshone River, so they sought while still early in the planning process to be as transparent as possible with the project, its methods, and goals.

The plan was to treat Eagle Creek with rotenone to remove wild brook trout over the course of two years and then release Yellowstone cutthroat trout into the stream. Eagle Creek is historically Yellowstone cutthroat trout habitat but has been lost as a result of the invasion by brook trout. As is common with such native trout restoration projects, the removal of non-natives was planned to take place above a natural barrier, a waterfall, approximately eight miles upstream from the confluence of Eagle Creek with the North Fork of the Shoshone River. The project area for the creek lies several miles in the backcountry of the Washakie Wilderness area of the Shoshone National Forest. As many as fifteen thousand brook trout were to be removed, which would then be replaced with five to ten thousand Yellowstone cutthroat trout. The potential loss of the wild brook trout population above the falls (although they would remain below the falls), rather than the use of rotenone, appears to have been the largest driver of resistance to the project.

The resistance to purging the brook trout was so strong in some quarters that county commissioners convened a special session to address the project. The writing was on the wall well before the meeting, with editorials in local newspapers decrying the loss of brook trout in Eagle Creek. I found the cultural acceptance of brook trout in local waters, as well as the lack of interest in seeing natives restored, both jarring and familiar. Although as an ecologist I was saddened by the resistance to the project, I had grown up in the Bighorn Basin and also understood the familiarity with, and emotional attachment to, the colorful little brook trout.

I first became aware of the proposed project in March of 2015. The project was dead by March of 2016, after county commissioners voted 3 to 1 to not support the project, even after the Game and Fish Department committed to the interim stocking of catchable-sized Yellowstone cutthroat trout to support fishing while completing the project. Those interim stocked natives would have been killed as additional treatments of rotenone were applied to the stream, to ensure that no brook trout survived to compete with the

Yellowstone cutthroat stocked at the conclusion of the project.[175] In the end, it mattered little that these additional monies and effort were available to address the perceived impacts to angling. Although the science was sound and the arguments persuasive, neither was enough to overcome the cultural identification with angling for non-native brook trout, an identification that has developed over several generations. Deep down I understood this sentiment, too, which has made me more aware than ever that the only way to counter such emotional attachments is by communicating both the local and global significance of native species conservation and restoration.

The failure of any single project, including the Eagle Creek restoration project, does not doom a conservation program. Every day there are conservation successes, and there are some even in the same locale where the Eagle Creek project failed. As I write this, Yellowstone cutthroat trout are being restored in the Bighorn Mountains of Rubyat and my home-waters. Not far from Eagle Creek, Yellowstone National Park's suppression of lake trout in Yellowstone Lake is beginning to take hold, and the lake's cutthroat trout population is hinting at a rebound; more and more lake trout are gillnetted every year, and the effectiveness of the program continues to increase. As the lake trout population declines, the number of Yellowstone cutthroat trout inhabiting the lake are beginning to inch upward. While both sides of this equation are encouraging, there is still work to be done. Eradication of lake trout from Yellowstone Lake isn't possible with today's technology, so it will require a sustained effort at gillnetting to continue to allow the lake's native cutthroat to hold on in their last stronghold.

Effective stewardship of natural resources, particularly on public lands, is stewardship that maintains the structure and function of the ecosystem through maintaining ecological resilience. As we have seen, for native trout, this means more than simply removing non-native trout and replacing them with natives. We must think broadly when planning and conducting conservation projects, asking hard questions of the long-term role of disturbances such as flood and wildfire. We must ask equally hard questions about whether resources used to stock non-natives and maintain wild fisheries would be better spent on maintaining and restoring native species to their historical habitat. Maintaining or enhancing the ecological resilience of forests, sagebrush steppe, and prairies ensures that we continue to move in a positive direction, as we reintroduce natives to aquatic habitats that have been lost over the last two centuries. But we must be careful to recognize that the gains made by these native trout conservation projects can be undermined at the ecosystem and landscape levels by the ongoing stocking of non-natives into the remaining range of natives that are still in peril and threatened with extinction. If we can be effective advocates for our native species, the rewards will reach far beyond the streambanks and resonate long after we have passed our homewaters on to the next generation.

Our cultural heritage is wrapped in the natural resources and lands that provide the ecological foundations of the landscapes in which we live. For me, connection to that landscape, its ecology, and its culture are best found through fly fishing. Although convincing a skeptical public that conservation of native trout should take precedence over the conservation of wild trout is a tough argument to make, it is an argument overwhelmingly supported by science and one that is only going to become more urgent in the years ahead. In the meantime, I will look forward to introducing my children to the sport of fly fishing and to sharing with them the important legacy and connection to nature that was passed down to me from my great-great-grandfather; one day soon we will be able to stand together knee-deep in Tensleep Creek, fishing for trout, just below the cabin Ruby Shultz built with his bare hands in the summer of 1916.

NOTES

1. There are numerous resources both in print and online that describe the geology of the Bighorn Basin; a good place to start is with David R. Lageson and Darwin Spearing's wonderfully engaging *Roadside Geology of Wyoming*.

2. For a detailed treatment of Theodore Roosevelt's efforts in conservation and natural resource management, see Edmund Morris's three-part biography. Volumes 1 and 2 (*The Rise of Theodore Roosevelt* and *Theodore Rex*) are particularly insightful about his outdoor and conservation exploits. Douglas Brinkley's biography of Roosevelt, *The Wilderness Warrior: Theodore Roosevelt and the Crusade for America*, is specifically built around Roosevelt's lifelong pursuit of natural resource conservation.

3. Brinkley, *Wilderness Warrior*.

4. See Roderick Frazier Nash's *Wilderness and the American Mind* for a detailed discussion of the American public's understanding of the concept of wilderness and the impact of the closing of the American frontier.

5. Daniel Kemmis, in *This Sovereign Land*, lays out the historical foundations underlying the perceived subjugation of western states through federal control of federal public lands. He also articulates a

vision for the central role that the people of the western states might play in a reorganization of public lands and their management in a more regional-centric scheme. Charles F. Wilkinson, in *Crossing the Next Meridian: Land, Water, and the Future of the West*, methodically reviews the historical foundations, enabling legislation, industry, culture, impacts, and conflicts associated with public land management. He details public land, water, and resource use in mining, ranching, forestry, salmon fisheries, and water development (such as dam and irrigation building), noting how industry and ecology have come into conflict as a result of federal legislation and policy, and he concludes by presenting a vision of resource management on public lands that seeks to reduce conflict.

6. Numerous attempts have been made, particularly in the Intermountain West, to wrest control of public lands—and their abundant natural resources—from the federal government and place them under state or local control. Some of the more recent manifestations include the Sagebrush Rebellion of the 1970s, the County Supremacy Movement of the 1980s, and the Wise Use Movement of the 1990s. Similar debates continue today in many western state legislatures, including those of Wyoming, Utah, Montana, Idaho, and Nevada. Such attempts are likely to fall well short of their goal, thanks to the Supremacy Clause of the U.S. Constitution. Robert Keiter and John Ruple, in "A Legal Analysis of the Transfer of Public Lands Movement"—a white paper analyzing the legal aspects of attempts by western states to seize control of federal public lands—concluded that the legal underpinnings of the argument supporting states' assertions of control over federal lands is constitutionally misconstrued and unsupported.

7. See Morris, *Theodore Rex*, and Brinkley, *Wilderness Warrior*, for depictions of the battles over the establishment of national forests, national monuments, and wildlife refuges.

8. This episode of Roosevelt's life is vividly described in Morris, *Rise of Theodore Roosevelt*, 213–34.

9. See Morris, *Rise of Theodore Roosevelt*, 278–97. It is worth noting that the sage-grouse harvested during this trip by Roosevelt and Merrifield are now the focus of intense conservation efforts throughout the western United States, in an attempt to prevent the species from being listed as endangered under the Endangered Species Act. Many western politicians and industry proponents believe that if the greater sage-grouse were to be listed, it would devastate both the mining and agricultural industries currently prevalent on public and private lands throughout the West. In September 2015, during the writing of this work, the U.S. Fish and Wildlife Service issued a decision that the greater sage-grouse was not in danger of extinction, in large part due to the efforts of the Bureau of Land Management and Forest Service and the commitments they made in numerous newly published resource management plans and forest management plans.

10. Schullery, "Theodore Roosevelt as an Angler."

11. This tale is told in Theodore Roosevelt's first-person *Hunting Trips of a Ranchman* and also recounted in Schullery's "Theodore Roosevelt as an Angler."

12. Schullery, "Theodore Roosevelt as an Angler."

13. Robert Behnke, in his seminal book *Trout and Salmon of North America*, provides a detailed review of the taxonomic classification and reclassification that has taken place over time, as a more thorough understanding of golden trout distribution and population relationships has evolved.

14. See Morris, *Rise of Theodore Roosevelt*.

15. Brinkley, in *Wilderness Warrior*, briefly touches on Roosevelt's belief that the "strenuous life" was a cure for the physical and social ailments of an urbanized society (350–51).

16. Behnke, "A Fishy 'Whodunit?" in *About Trout*, 217–19.

17. Livingston Stone has often been credited with being the first person in the United States to propagate and distribute rainbow trout outside their native range. However, Anders Halverson, in ch. 3 of *An Entirely Synthetic Fish*, instead gives credit to the Ornithological and Piscatorial Acclimatizing Society of California for first stocking rainbow trout outside their native range.

18. Halverson, *An Entirely Synthetic Fish*, 30.

19. Varley and Schullery, *Yellowstone Fishes*, 94.

20. Behnke, "From Hatcheries to Habitat? Look Again," in *About Trout*, 150.

21. Behnke, "From Hatcheries to Habitat? Look Again," in *About Trout*, 149.

22. The quotes are from Wiley, *Wyoming Fish Management, 1869–1993*, 2–3.

23. Personal communication, Sam Hochhalter and Jason Burckhardt, Wyoming Game and Fish Department, Cody, WY, December 15, 2016.

24. The Boutelle quote is from Varley, "A History of Fish Stocking Activities in Yellowstone," p. II.

25. Varley, "A History of Fish Stocking Activities in Yellowstone."

26. Varley and Schullery, *Yellowstone Fishes.*

27. Varley, "A History of Fish Stocking Activities in Yellowstone."

28. Munro, McMahon, and Ruzycki, "Where Did They Come From?"

29. See Varley, "A History of Fish Stocking Activities in Yellowstone," 15.

30. Varley and Schullery, *Yellowstone Fishes.*

31. Koel et al., "Yellowstone Fisheries and Aquatic Sciences: Annual Report, 2009–2010."

32. For additional information on hybridization that results in species like the splake and tiger trout, see Behnke, *Trout and Salmon of North America*, 270, 276, 279.

33. Bahls, "The Status of Fish Populations."

34. Pister, "Wilderness Fish Stocking"; Pilliod and Peterson, "Local and Landscape Effects of Introduced Trout."

35. Pister, "Wilderness Fish Stocking"; Pilliod and Peterson, "Local and Landscape Effects of Introduced Trout."

36. Behnke, *Trout and Salmon of North America*, 199.

37. Pister, "Wilderness Fish Stocking"; Pilliod and Peterson. "Local and Landscape Effects of Introduced Trout."

38. Behnke, *Trout and Salmon of North America*, 143.

39. Behnke, *Trout and Salmon of North America*, 168.

40. For a brief description of the geological forces that have shaped the possibility of a single creek draining to both sides of the Continental Divide, see Lageson and Spearing, *Roadside Geology of Wyoming*, 225–26.

41. For a fascinating story of the movement of the species across the Continental Divide, see Behnke, *Trout and Salmon of North America*, 169.

42. Varley and Schullery, *Yellowstone Fishes*, 8.

43. Behnke, *Trout and Salmon of North America*, 176.

44. Behnke, *Trout and Salmon of North America*, 175.

45. May, Albeke, and Horton, "Range-Wide Status of Yellowstone Cutthroat Trout," 9.

46. Personal communication, Sam Hochhalter and Jason Burckhardt, Wyoming Game and Fish Department, Cody, WY, December 15, 2016.

47. May, Albeke, and Horton. "Range-Wide Status of Yellowstone Cutthroat Trout."

48. Behnke, *Trout and Salmon of North America*, 195–99.

49. Metcalf et al., "Historical Stocking Data and 19th Century DNA."

50. Behnke, *Trout and Salmon of North America*, 195–99.

51. Metcalf et al., "Historical Stocking Data and 19th Century DNA."

52. U.S. Fish and Wildlife Service, "Endangered and Threatened Wildlife and Plants; 12-Month Finding to List Rio Grande Cutthroat Trout."

53. For further background on the attempts to list the Yellowstone cutthroat trout under the Endangered Species Act, see U.S. Fish and Wildlife Service, "Endangered and Threatened Wildlife and Plants; 12-Month Finding to List the Yellowstone Cutthroat Trout."

54. May, Albeke, and Horton, "Range-Wide Status of Yellowstone Cutthroat Trout."

55. Behnke, "Paiute Cutthroat," in *About Trout*, 81.

56. The impacts of stocking non-native trout into the range of the Yellowstone cutthroat trout are well addressed in Robert E. Gresswell, "Biology, Status, and Management of the Yellowstone Cutthroat Trout." For a broader discussion on the impacts of hybridization of cutthroat trout with other species stocked into their habitat, see Behnke, *Trout and Salmon of North America*, 139–48.

57. Quoted in the introduction of Behnke, *About Trout*, 2.

58. Wilkinson, *Crossing the Next Meridian*.

59. Wilkinson, *Crossing the Next Meridian*.

60. Whittlesey, "Of Fairies' Wings and Fish"; Varley and Schullery, *Yellowstone Fishes*.

61. Behnke, "We're Putting Them Back Alive," in *About Trout*, 117–29.

62. Behnke, "From Hatcheries to Habitat? Look Again," in *About Trout*, 152.

63. Behnke, providing some additional commentary in *About Trout* on his original article, notes that there is an "unreasonable subsidy" when, at

the time of that writing, 30 percent or more of fisheries budgets were dedicated to raising catchable-sized trout. In light of today's era of reduced government budgets, the issue has become even more acute, as fishery policies and programs increasingly compete with one another for scarce and declining dollars.

64.   It is important to note that the Yellowstone cutthroat trout, which I have used as my example for native species conservation, has also been stocked outside of its native range, in the same way that rainbow, brook, brown, and lake trout have been. Nevertheless the Yellowstone cutthroat trout has diminished throughout a considerable portion of its own range, as non-natives and other stressors have had an impact on the species.

65.   Fish Management Chemicals Subcommittee, "Maintaining North America's Healthy Native Aquatic Ecosystems."

66.   Finlayson et al., *Rotenone Use in Fisheries Management.*

67.   Halverson, *An Entirely Synthetic Fish*, 96–99.

68.   Halverson provides an exacting account of this project and its unanticipated impacts, along with the views of opponents and proponents of the project alike, in *An Entirely Synthetic Fish*, 94–113.

69.   Rice, "Rare Native Fish Found in Utah."

70.   Behnke, *Trout and Salmon of North America*, 73–74.

71.   Behnke, *Trout and Salmon of North America*, 140.

72.   Kanda, Leary, and Allendorf, "Evidence of Introgressive Hybridization."

73. Behnke, *Trout and Salmon of North America*, 149–53.

74. Behnke, *Trout and Salmon of North America*, 151–53.

75. Behnke, *Trout and Salmon of North America*, 160.

76. Muhlfeld et al., "Hybridization Rapidly Reduces Fitness."

77. Muhlfeld et al., "Hybridization Rapidly Reduces Fitness."

78. Behnke, *About Trout*, 123.

79. Kolbert, *Sixth Extinction*.

80. The information on moose translocation from the Jackson Hole, Wyoming, area to the Bighorn Mountains in Wyoming is gleaned from Wyoming Game and Fish Department, *Bighorn Herd Unit M313*, 419.

81. Collen and Gibson, "General Ecology of Beavers."

82. Collen and Gibson, "General Ecology of Beavers."

83. Collen and Gibson, "General Ecology of Beavers"; Hägglund and Sjöberg, "Effects of Beaver Dams."

84. Gregory et al., "An Ecosystem Perspective of Riparian Zones."

85. Gregory et al., "An Ecosystem Perspective of Riparian Zones."

86. Mech and Boitani, *Wolves: Behavior, Ecology, and Conservation*.

87. Boitani, "Wolf Conservation and Recovery," 317–40.

88. Fritts et al., "Wolves and Humans."

89. Fritts et al., "Wolves and Humans."

90. Fritts et al., "Wolves and Humans."

91. Boitani, "Wolf Conservation and Recovery."

92. Citing Curnow, "The History of the Eradication of the Wolf in Montana," and McIntyre, "Review and Assessment of Possibilities for Protecting the Cutthroat Trout," in Boitani, "Wolf Conservation and Recovery."

93. Leopold, *Sand County Almanac*, 138–39.

94. Citing Jones, *Wolf Mountains*, in Fritts et al., "Wolves and Humans."

95. Boitani, "Wolf Conservation and Recovery."

96. Citing Fischer, *Wolf Wars*, in Fritts et al., "Wolves and Humans."

97. The capture of gray wolves in Canada for reintroduction of the species into Wyoming and Idaho resulted in opponents of the reintroduction (and opponents of wolves in general) declaring that the reintroduced wolves were non-natives because they were captured across the U.S.-Canadian boundary—an incorrect label that I still see being applied to wolves today in the Greater Yellowstone Ecosystem. It is unlikely that the purpose in labeling the Canadian captured wolves as non-natives was due to a belief that, prior to extermination efforts, wolf populations had neatly partitioned themselves on each side of a political boundary; rather, it is best understood as one arrow, among many, aimed at undermining the scientific foundation of the reintroduction effort.

98. A number of other federal agencies, including the U.S. Department of Defense and the U.S. Bureau of Reclamation, also manage lands within the public domain but to a much lesser extent than the "big four."

99. A tremendous amount of literature examines the rural/urban divide, as it applies to natural resource management. The two following works describe the relationship as it applies to the management of wolves: Martin A. Nie, *Beyond Wolves*; Fritts et al., "Wolves and Humans."

100. Layzer, *The Environmental Case*, 159–90; Switzer, "Public and Private Lands."

101. To get a sense of the manner in which politics, policy, and science influenced the delisting process for the gray wolf in the Northern Rockies, see the short online National Park Service article "Wolf Restoration Continued."

102. Leopold, *Sand County Almanac*, 262.

103. Peterson and Ciucci, "Wolf as a Carnivore."

104. For an examination of the long-term condition of both aspen and willow communities, including the decline of both species following the extirpation of wolves and subsequent growth of the elk herds, see Kay and Wagner, "Historic Condition of Woody Vegetation." For studies that look at the ecological changes that have taken place since the reintroduction of wolves to Yellowstone, see Painter et al., "Recovering Aspen Follow Changing Elk Dynamics," and Bilyeu, Cooper, and Hobbs, "Water Tables Constrain Height Recovery of Willow."

105. Hebblewhite et al., "Human Activity Mediates a Trophic Cascade."

106. Hebblewhite et al., "Human Activity Mediates a Trophic Cascade."

107. Wolf, Cooper, and Hobbs, "Hydrologic Regime and Herbivory"; Bilyeu, Cooper, and Hobbs, "Water Tables Constrain Height Recovery of Willow."

108. For a brief review of the literature and logic that surrounds wolf harvest as part of a larger wolf conservation strategy, see Boitani, "Wolf Conservation and Recovery," 336–37.

109. For an excellent article that provides a review of numerous ecosystem types that are influenced, whether positively or negatively, by disturbance, see Folke et al., "Regime Shifts, Resilience, and Biodiversity." For book-length examinations of the role of disturbance on ecological resilience, see Gunderson, Holling, and Light, *Barriers and Bridges to the Renewal of Ecosystems and Institutions*, and Walker and Salt, *Resilience Thinking*.

110. For an understanding of the way in which fire shapes different ecosystem types in the northern Rocky Mountains, I highly recommend Dennis Knight's *Mountains and Plains*. I have not yet had the opportunity to peruse the recently published second edition, but I'm certain that it is as well written and informative as the first. For another useful discussion of how different fire regimes and the policy of fire suppression influences montane forests, see Keane and Key, "CCE Fire Regimes and Their Management."

111. C. S. Holling's seminal work on ecological resilience, "The Resilience of Terrestrial Ecosystems: Local Surprise and Global Change," provides a delineation between slow, intermediate, and fast variables within a variety of ecosystems. The key to this concept is that while some processes such as a fire are—in and of themselves—fast, the nutrient cycling that results from the release and the regeneration of the burned-over stand is, within the context of ecosystem processes, slow. Thus it is important to

appreciate the speed at which different ecological processes take place, in order to prevent losing sight of the important role that disturbance plays in an ecosystem. For an important contextualization and application of the concepts related to ecosystem processes, see Chapin, Kofinas, and Folke, *Principles of Ecosystem Stewardship.*

112. Bigler, Kulakowski, and Veblen, "Multiple Disturbance Interactions and Drought Influence Fire Severity."

113. As with all things ecological, there are nearly always numerous influences that result in an observable outcome. For mountain pine beetle outbreaks and their impacts, it is not just the outbreak itself that results in the death of large stands of trees; often the conditions of the forest itself prior to and during the outbreak play an important role as well. For an understanding of the dynamics of mountain pine beetles, see Logan and Powell, "Ghost Forests, Global Warming," which provides an excellent review of the life cycle of the mountain pine beetle and the beetle's coevolved relationship with western pine forests. For a detailed understanding of the interactions of historical and contemporary disturbances and their relationship to the current mountain pine beetle epidemic sweeping through western North America, I recommend Kulakowski and Jarvis, "Influence of Mountain Pine Beetle Outbreaks and Drought," and Bigler, Kulakowski, and Veblen, "Multiple Disturbance Interactions and Drought." Taken together, these two articles provide a detailed understanding of the role that mountain pine beetles play in forest dynamics.

114. Knight, *Mountains and Plains.*

115. Bigler, Kulakowski, and Veblen, "Multiple Disturbance Interactions and Drought."

116. Logan and Powell, "Ghost Forests, Global Warming."

117. For an excellent review not only of the impacts of fire-related disturbance on native trout but also of how climate change may well change fire regimes and have possible direct and indirect impacts on trout, see Luce et al., "Climate Change, Forests, Fire, Water, and Fish."

118. Varley and Schullery, "Fires and Fish," in *Yellowstone Fishes.*

119. Documentation of the epic fires of 1910 has been both broad and deep, spanning numerous forms of written accounts that include biographies, detailed research, recorded personal accounts, and PBS documentaries, to name only a few. Some of the most worthwhile and enjoyable materials include Timothy Egan's *The Big Burn,* Stephen J. Pyne's *Year of the Fires*, and the PBS documentary *The Big Burn.*

120. Knight, *Mountains and Plains.*

121. A robust body of ecological literature surrounds the debate between linear and nonlinear ecosystem dynamics, as well as the concept of multiple equilibria. For our purposes, I will recommend three works that would provide a great starting point for understanding the debate. The first is C. S. Holling's seminal work on ecological resilience, "The Resilience of Terrestrial Ecosystems." The second is Brian Walker and David Salt's *Resilience Thinking*, a short, well-written, and easily understood book on the subject, which includes case studies. The third is Holling's article "Engineering Resilience versus Ecological Resilience," which directly addresses the two different ways in which people (including scientists) view how ecosystems respond following a disturbance.

122. Holling, "Resilience of Terrestrial Ecosystems"; Holling, "Engineering Resilience versus Ecological Resilience."

123. Holling, "Resilience and Stability of Ecological Systems"; Holling, "Resilience of Terrestrial Ecosystems."

124. While the study of social-ecological resilience and the role humans play in consuming ecosystem goods and services is increasing in scope and depth, a good starting place for understanding the concept is Lance H. Gunderson and C. S. Holling's *Panarchy*.

125. Varley and Schullery, *Yellowstone Fishes*, 18–19.

126. Varley and Schullery, "Yellowstone Lake and Its Cutthroat Trout."

127. Barbee quoted in Milstein, "Eco-Vandalism."

128. Varley quoted in Associated Press, "Lake Trout Threaten Yellowstone."

129. McIntyre, "Review and Assessment of Possibilities for Protecting the Cutthroat Trout."

130. McIntyre, "Review and Assessment of Possibilities for Protecting the Cutthroat Trout."

131. Koel et al., "Yellowstone Fisheries and Aquatic Sciences: Annual Report, 2009–2010."

132. Koel et al., "Yellowstone Fisheries and Aquatic Sciences: Annual Report, 2006."

133. Koel et al., "Nonnative Lake Trout."

134. Koel et al., "Nonnative Lake Trout."

135. Koel et al., "Yellowstone Fisheries and Aquatic Sciences: Annual Report, 2011."

136. Koel et al., "Yellowstone Fisheries and Aquatic Sciences: Annual Report, 2011."

137. Bigelow et al., "Protection of Native Yellowstone Cutthroat Trout."

138. Ruzycki, Beauchamp, and Yule, "Effects of Introduced Lake Trout."

139. Varley and Schullery, "Yellowstone Lake Crisis."

140. Tronstad et al., "Introduced Lake Trout."

141. Quoted in Koel et al., "Nonnative Lake Trout," 16.

142. Kaeding, Boltz, and Carty, "Lake Trout Discovered in Yellowstone Lake," cited in Munro, McMahon, and Ruzycki, "Where Did They Come From?"

143. Munro, McMahon, and Ruzycki, "Where Did They Come From?"

144. Varley, "A History of Fish Stocking Activities."

145. Gresswell, "Scientific Panel Evaluation."

146. Bigelow et al., "Protection of Native Yellowstone Cutthroat Trout."

147. Koel et al., "Yellowstone Fisheries and Aquatic Sciences: Annual Report, 2009–2010."

148. Schullery and Varley, "Cutthroat Trout and the Yellowstone Lake Ecosystem."

149. Varley and Schullery, "Yellowstone Lake and Its Cutthroat Trout."

150. Reinhart and Mattson, "Bear Use of Cutthroat Trout Spawning Streams."

151. Hoskins, "Yellowstone Lake Tributary Study."

152. Haroldson et al., "Changing Numbers of Spawning Cutthroat Trout."

153. Logan, MacFarlane, and Willcox, "Whitebark Pine Vulnerability."

154. Bockino and Tinker, "Interactions of White Pine Blister Rust and Mountain Pine Beetle."

155. Tomback and Achuff, "Blister Rust and Western Forest Biodiversity."

156. Tomback and Achuff, "Blister Rust and Western Forest Biodiversity."

157. Tomback and Achuff, "Blister Rust and Western Forest Biodiversity."

158. Bockino and Tinker, "Interactions of White Pine Blister Rust and Mountain Pine Beetle."

159. Tomback and Achuff, "Blister Rust and Western Forest Biodiversity."

160. Krugman and Jenkinson, "*Pinus* L. Pine," cited in McCaughey and Tomback, "Natural Regeneration Process."

161. McCaughey and Tomback, "Natural Regeneration Process."

162. Tomback, "Dispersal of Whitebark Pine Seeds by Clark's Nutcracker."

163. For additional information on the role of whitebark pine in food webs, see Tomback and Kendall, "Biodiversity Losses."

164. Hutchins and Lanner, "Central Role of Clark's Nutcracker."

165. Hutchins and Lanner, "Central Role of Clark's Nutcracker."

166. Tomback, "Dispersal of Whitebark Pine Seeds by Clark's Nutcracker."

167. Tomback and Achuff, "Blister Rust and Western Forest Biodiversity."

168. See Knight, *Mountains and Plains*, 223–24.

169. Bockino and Tinker, "Interactions of White Pine Blister Rust and Mountain Pine Beetle."

170. Arno, "Community Types and Natural Disturbance Processes."

171. Arno, "Community Types and Natural Disturbance Processes."

172. U.S. Fish and Wildlife Service, "Endangered and Threatened Wildlife and Plants; 12-Month Finding on a Petition to List *Pinus albicaulis*."

173. Warwell, Rehfeldt, and Crookston, "Modeling Contemporary Climate Profiles of Whitebark Pine."

174. McLellan et al., *Living Planet Report 2014*.

175. Freedman, "Eagle Creek Trout Plan"; Freedman, "G&F Won't Pursue N. Fork Trout Plan."

BIBLIOGRAPHY

Arno, Stephen F. "Community Types and Natural Disturbance Processes." In *Whitebark Pine Communities: Ecology and Restoration*, edited by Diana F. Tomback, Stephen F. Arno, and Robert E. Keane, 74–88. Washington, DC: Island Press, 2001.

Associated Press. "Lake Trout Threaten Yellowstone Wildlife Officials to Lay Down Gill Nets in Bid to Stop Invasion." *Spokesman-Review*, July 9, 1996.

Bahls, Peter. "The Status of Fish Populations and Management of High Mountain Lakes in the Western United States." *Northwest Science* 66, no. 3 (1992): 183–93.

Behnke, Robert J. *About Trout: The Best of Robert J. Behnke from* Trout *Magazine*. Guilford, CT: Lyons Press, 2007.

Behnke, Robert J. *Trout and Salmon of North America*. New York: Free Press, 2002.

Bigelow, Patricia E., Todd M. Koel, Dan Mahony, Brian Ertel, Barb Rowdon, and S. Thomas Olliff. "Protection of Native Yellowstone Cutthroat Trout in Yellowstone Lake—Yellowstone National Park Wyoming." Yellowstone National Park, WY: NPS Aquatic Resources Center, 2003.

Bigler, Christof, Dominik Kulakowski, and Thomas T. Veblen. "Multiple Disturbance Interactions and Drought Influence Fire Severity in Rocky Mountain Subalpine Forests." *Ecology* 86, no. 11 (2005): 3018–29.

Bilyeu, Danielle M., David J. Cooper, and N. Thompson Hobbs. "Water Tables Constrain Height Recovery of Willow on Yellowstone's Northern Range." *Ecological Applications* 18, no. 1 (2008): 80–92.

Bockino, Nancy K., and Daniel B. Tinker. "Interactions of White Pine Blister Rust and Mountain Pine Beetle in Whitebark Pine Ecosystems in the Southern Greater Yellowstone Area." *Natural Areas Journal* 32 (2012): 31–40.

Boitani, Luigi. "Wolf Conservation and Recovery." In *Wolves: Behavior, Ecology, and Conservation*, edited by L. David Mech and Luigi Boitani, 317–40. Chicago: University of Chicago Press, 2003.

Brinkley, Douglas. *The Wilderness Warrior: Theodore Roosevelt and the Crusade for America*. New York: Harper Perennial, 2009.

Chapin, F. Stuart, III, Gary P. Kofinas, and Carl Folke. *Principles of Ecosystem Stewardship: Resilience-Based Natural Resource Management in a Changing World*. New York: Springer Science + Business Media, 2009.

Collen, P., and R. J. Gibson. "The General Ecology of Beavers (*Castor* spp.), as Related to Their Influence on Stream Ecosystems and Riparian Habitats, and the Subsequent Effects on Fish—A Review." *Reviews in Fish Biology and Fisheries* 10 (2001): 439–61.

Curnow, Edward. "The History of the Eradication of the Wolf in Montana." Master's thesis, University of Montana, Missoula, MT, 1969.

Egan, Timothy. *The Big Burn: Teddy Roosevelt and the Fire That Saved America*. Boston: Houghton Mifflin Harcourt, 2009.

Finlayson, Brian J., Rosalie A. Schnick, Richard L. Cailteux, Leo DeMong, William D Horton, William McClay, Charles W. Thompson, and Gregory J. Tichacek. *Rotenone Use in Fisheries Management: Administrative and Technical Guidelines Manual.* Bethesda, MD: American Fisheries Society, 2000.

Fischer, Hank. *Wolf Wars.* Helena, MT: Falcon Press, 1995.

Fish Management Chemicals Subcommittee. "Maintaining North America's Healthy Native Aquatic Ecosystems: Rotenone's Role in Eradicating Invasive Fishes, Parasites, and Disease." Bethesda, MD: American Fisheries Society, 2010.

Folke, Carl, Steve Carpenter, Brian Walker, Marten Scheffer, Thomas Elmqvist, Lance Gunderson, and C. S. Holling. "Regime Shifts, Resilience, and Biodiversity in Ecosystem Management." *Annual Review Ecology Evolution Systematics* 35 (2004): 557–81.

Freedman, Lew. "Eagle Creek Trout Plan Would Add Temporary Fishery." *Cody Enterprise*, March 2, 2016.

Freedman, Lew. "G&F Won't Pursue N. Fork Trout Plan." *Cody Enterprise*, March 21, 2016.

Fritts, Steven H., Robert O. Stephenson, Robert D. Hayes, and Luigi Boitani. "Wolves and Humans." In *Wolves: Behavior, Ecology, and Conservation*, edited by L. David Mech and Luigi Boitani, 289–316. Chicago: University of Chicago Press, 2003.

Gregory, Stanley V., Frederick J. Swanson, W. Arthur McKee, and Kenneth W. Cummins. "An Ecosystem Perspective of Riparian Zones: Focus on Links between Land and Water." *Bioscience* 41, no. 8 (1991): 540–51.

Gresswell, Robert E. "Biology, Status, and Management of the Yellowstone Cutthroat Trout." *North American Journal of Fisheries Management* 31 (2011): 782–812.

Gresswell, Robert E. "Scientific Panel Evaluation of the National Park Service Lake Trout Suppression Program in Yellowstone Lake, August 25–29, 2008. Final Report." Bozeman, MT: USGS Northern Rocky Mountain Science Center, 2009.

Gunderson, Lance H., and C. S. Holling, eds. *Panarchy: Understanding Transformations in Human and Natural Systems*. Washington, DC: Island Press, 2002.

Gunderson, Lance H., C. S. Holling, and Stephen S. Light, eds. *Barriers and Bridges to the Renewal of Ecosystems and Institutions*. New York: Columbia University Press, 1995.

Hägglund, Åsa, and Göran Sjöberg. "Effects of Beaver Dams on the Fish Fauna of Forest Streams." *Forest Ecology and Management* 115 (1999): 259–66.

Halverson, Anders. *An Entirely Synthetic Fish: How Rainbow Trout Beguiled America and Overran the World*. New Haven, CT: Yale University Press, 2010.

Haroldson, Mark A., Kerry A. Gunther, Daniel P. Reinhart, Shannon R. Podruzny, Chris Cegelski, Lisette Waits, Travis Wyman, and Jeremiah Smith. "Changing Numbers of Spawning Cutthroat Trout in Tributary Streams of Yellowstone Lake and Estimates of Grizzly Bears from DNA." *Ursus* 16, no. 2 (2005): 167–80.

Hebblewhite, Mark, Clifford A. White, Clifford G. Nietvelt, John A. McKenzie, Tomas E. Hurd, John M. Fryxell, Suzanne E. Bayley, and

Paul C. Paquet. "Human Activity Mediates a Trophic Cascade Caused by Wolves." *Ecology* 86, no. 8 (2005): 2135–44.

Holling, C. S. "Engineering Resilience versus Ecological Resilience." In *Engineering within Ecological Constraints*, edited by Peter C. Schulze, 31–44. Washington, DC: National Academies Press, 1996.

Holling, C. S. "Resilience and Stability of Ecological Systems." *Annual Review of Ecology and Systematics* 4 (1973): 1–23.

Holling, C. S. "The Resilience of Terrestrial Ecosystems: Local Surprise and Global Change." In *Sustainable Development of the Biosphere*, edited by William C. Clark and R. E. Munn, 292–317. Cambridge, UK: Cambridge University Press, 1986.

Hoskins, W. P. "Yellowstone Lake Tributary Study: Interagency Grizzly Bear Study Team." Unpublished report. Bozeman, MT, 1975.

Hutchins, Harry E., and Ronald M. Lanner. "The Central Role of Clark's Nutcracker in the Dispersal and Establishment of Whitebark Pine." *Oecologia* 55 (1982): 192–201.

Jones, Karen R. *Wolf Mountains: A History of Wolves Along the Great Divide*. Calgary, Alberta: University of Calgary Press, 2002.

Kaeding, Lynn R., Glenn D. Boltz, and Daniel G. Carty. "Lake Trout Discovered in Yellowstone Lake Threaten Native Cutthroat Trout." *Fisheries* 21, no. 3 (1996): 16–20.

Kanda, Naohisa, Robb F. Leary, and Fred W. Allendorf. "Evidence of Introgressive Hybridization between Bull Trout and Brook Trout." *Transactions of the American Fisheries Society* 131 (2002): 772–82.

Kay, C. E., and F. H. Wagner. "Historic Condition of Woody Vegetation on Yellowstone's Northern Range: A Critical Evaluation of the 'Natural Regulation' Paradigm." In *Proceedings of the First Scientific Conference on the Greater Yellowstone Ecosystem. Technical Report*, edited by D. G. Despain, 151–69. Denver, CO: National Park Service, 1994.

Keane, Robert E., and Carl Key. "CCE Fire Regimes and Their Management." In *Sustaining Rocky Mountain Landscapes: Science, Policy, and Management for the Crown of the Continent Ecosystem*, edited by Tony Prato and Dan Fagre, 201–12. Washington, DC: Resources for the Future, 2007.

Keiter, Robert B., and John C. Ruple. "A Legal Analysis of the Transfer of Public Lands Movement." Stegner Center White Paper No. 2014-2. Wallace Stegner Center for Land, Resources, and the Environment, University of Utah, S. J. Quinney College of Law, October 27, 2014.

Kemmis, Daniel. *This Sovereign Land: A New Vision for Governing the West*. Washington, DC: Island Press, 2001.

Knight, Dennis H. *Mountains and Plains: The Ecology of Wyoming Landscapes*. New Haven, CT: Yale University Press, 1994.

Koel, Todd M., Jeffrey L. Arnold, Patricia E. Bigelow, Philip D. Doepke, Brian D. Ertel, and Michael E. Ruhl. "Yellowstone Fisheries and Aquatic Sciences: Annual Report, 2006." Yellowstone National Park, WY: National Park Service, Yellowstone Center for Resources, 2007.

Koel, Todd M., Jeffrey L. Arnold, Patricia E. Bigelow, Philip D. Doepke, Brian D. Ertel, and Michael E. Ruhl. "Yellowstone Fisheries and Aquatic Sciences: Annual Report, 2009–2010." Yellowstone National Park, WY: National Park Service, Yellowstone Center for Resources, 2012.

Koel, Todd M., Jeffrey L. Arnold, Patricia E. Bigelow, Philip D. Doepke, Brian D. Ertel, and Michael E. Ruhl. "Yellowstone Fisheries and Aquatic Sciences: Annual Report, 2011." Yellowstone National Park, WY: National Park Service, Yellowstone Center for Resources, 2012.

Koel, Todd M., Patricia E. Bigelow, Philip D. Doepke, Brian D. Ertel, and Dan L. Mahony. "Nonnative Lake Trout Result in Yellowstone Cutthroat Trout Decline and Impacts to Bears and Anglers." *Fisheries* 30, no. 11 (2005): 10–19.

Kolbert, Elizabeth. *The Sixth Extinction: An Unnatural History*. London: A&C Black, 2014.

Krugman S. L., and J. L. Jenkinson. *Pinus* L. Pine. In *Seeds of Woody Plants in the United States*, edited by C. S. Schopmeyer, 598–638. USDA Forest Service, Agricultural Handbook 450, Washington, DC.

Kulakowski, Dominik, and Daniel Jarvis. "The Influence of Mountain Pine Beetle Outbreaks and Drought on Severe Wildfires in Northwestern Colorado and Southern Wyoming: A Look at the Past Century." *Forest Ecology and Management* 262 (2011): 1686–96.

Lageson, David R., and Darwin Spearing. *Roadside Geology of Wyoming*. Missoula, MT: Mountain Press, 1988.

Layzer, Judith A. *The Environmental Case: Translating Values into Policy*. 2nd ed. Washington, DC: CQ Press, 2006.

Leopold, Aldo. *A Sand County Almanac with Essays on Conservation from Round River*. New York: Ballantine Books, 1986.

Logan, Jesse A., William W. MacFarlane, and Louisa Willcox. "Whitebark Pine Vulnerability to Climate-Driven Mountain Pine Beetle Disturbance in the Greater Yellowstone Ecosystem." *Ecological Applications* 20, no. 4 (2010): 895–902.

Logan, Jesse A., and James A. Powell. "Ghost Forests, Global Warming, and the Mountain Pine Beetle (*Coleoptera: Scolytidae*)." *American Entomologist*, Fall 2001: 160–72.

Luce, Charles, Penny Morgan, Kathleen Dwire, Daniel Isaak, Zachary Holden, and Bruce Rieman. "Climate Change, Forests, Fire, Water, and Fish: Building Resilient Landscapes, Streams, and Managers." General Technical Report RMRS-GTR-290. Fort Collins, CO: USDA Forest Service, Rocky Mountain Research Station, 2012.

May, Bruce E., Shannon E. Albeke, and Travis Horton. "Range-Wide Status of Yellowstone Cutthroat Trout (*Oncorhynchus clarkii bouvieri*): 2006. Prepared for Yellowstone Cutthroat Trout Interagency Coordination Group." Helena, MT: Montana Department of Fish, Wildlife, and Parks, 2007.

McCaughey, Ward W., and Diana F. Tomback. "The Natural Regeneration Process." In *Whitebark Pine Communities: Ecology and Restoration*, edited by Diana F. Tomback, Stephen F. Arno, and Robert E. Keane, 105–20. Washington, DC: Island Press, 2001.

McIntyre, John D. "Review and Assessment of Possibilities for Protecting the Cutthroat Trout of Yellowstone Lake from Introduced Lake Trout." In *The Yellowstone Lake Crisis: Confronting a Lake Trout Invasion. A Report to the Director of the National Park Service*, 28–33. Yellowstone National Park, WY: Yellowstone Center for Resources, 1995.

McLellan, Richard, Leena Iyengar, Barney Jeffries, and Natasja Oerlemans, eds. *Living Planet Report 2014: Species and Spaces, People and Places*. Gland, Switzerland: World Wildlife Fund, 2014.

Mech, L. David, and Luigi Boitani, eds. *Wolves: Behavior, Ecology, and Conservation*. Chicago: University of Chicago Press, 2003.

Metcalf, J. L., S. Love Stowell, C. M. Kennedy, K. B. Rogers, D. McDonald, J. Epp, K. Keepers, et al. "Historical Stocking Data and 19th Century DNA Reveal Human-Induced Changes to Native Diversity and Distribution of Cutthroat Trout." *Molecular Ecology* 21, no. 21 (2012): 5194–207.

Milstein, Michael. "Eco-Vandalism: Alien Trout Play Havoc in Yellowstone." *High Country News*, September 19, 1994.

Morris, Edmund. *The Rise of Theodore Roosevelt*. New York: Random House, 2010.

Morris, Edmund. *Theodore Rex*. New York: Random House, 2001.

Muhlfeld, Clint C., Steven T. Kalinowski, Thomas E. McMahon, Mark L. Taper, Sally Painter, Robb F. Leary, and Fred W. Allendorf. "Hybridization Rapidly Reduces Fitness of a Native Trout in the Wild." *Biology Letters* 5 (2009): 328–31.

Munro, Andrew R., Thomas E. McMahon, and James R. Ruzycki. "Where Did They Come From? Natural Chemical Markers Identify Source and Date of Lake Trout Introduction in Yellowstone Lake." *Yellowstone Science* 14, no. 2 (2006): 4–12.

Nash, Roderick Frazier. *Wilderness and the American Mind*. 4th ed. New Haven, CT: Yale University Press, 2001.

National Park Service. Yellowstone National Park. "Wolf Restoration Continued." www.nps.gov/yell/learn/nature/wolfrestorationinfo.htm. Accessed June 1, 2017.

Nie, Martin A. *Beyond Wolves: The Politics of Wolf Recovery and Management.* Minneapolis: University of Minnesota Press, 2003.

Painter, Luke E., Robert L. Beschta, Eric J. Larsen, and William J. Ripple. "Recovering Aspen Follow Changing Elk Dynamics in Yellowstone: Evidence of a Trophic Cascade." *Ecology* 96, no. 1 (2015): 252–63.

PBS (Public Broadcasting Service). *The Big Burn* (*American Experience* series). Written and directed by Stephen Ives. Aired February 3, 2015.

Peterson, Rolf O., and Paolo Ciucci. "The Wolf as a Carnivore." In *Wolves: Behavior, Ecology, and Conservation*, edited by L. David Mech and Luigi Boitani, 104–30. Chicago: University of Chicago Press, 2003.

Pilliod, David S., and Charles R. Peterson. "Local and Landscape Effects of Introduced Trout on Amphibians in Historically Fishless Watersheds." *Ecosystems* 4 (2001): 322–33.

Pister, Edwin P. "Wilderness Fish Stocking: History and Perspective." *Ecosystems* 4 (2001): 279–86.

Pyne, Stephen J. *Year of the Fires: The Story of the Great Fires of 1910.* New York: Viking, 2001.

Reinhart, Daniel P., and David J. Mattson. "Bear Use of Cutthroat Trout Spawning Streams in Yellowstone National Park." In *Bears: Their Biology and Management.* Papers of the Eighth International Conference on Bear Research and Management, vol. 8 (1990): 343–50.

Rice, Jeff. "Rare Native Fish Found in Utah, Then Poisoned by Mistake." *High Country News*, November 27, 1995.

Roosevelt, Theodore. *Hunting Trips of a Ranchman and the Wilderness Hunter.* New York: Modern Library, 2000.

Ruzycki, James R., David A. Beauchamp, and Daniel L. Yule. "Effects of Introduced Lake Trout on Native Cutthroat Trout in Yellowstone Lake." *Ecological Applications* 13, no. 1 (2003): 23–37.

Schullery, Paul. "Theodore Roosevelt as an Angler." *American Fly Fisher* 9, no. 3 (1982): 20–27.

Schullery, Paul, and John D. Varley. "Cutthroat Trout and the Yellowstone Lake Ecosystem." In *The Yellowstone Lake Crisis: Confronting a Lake Trout Invasion: A Report to the Director of the National Park Service*, edited by John D. Varley and Paul Schullery, 12–21. Yellowstone National Park, WY: Yellowstone Center for Resources, 1995.

Switzer, Jacqueline Vaughn. "Public and Private Lands." In *Environmental Politics: Domestic and Global Dimensions*, 105–36. Belmont, CA: Wadsworth, 2004.

Tomback, Diana F. "Dispersal of Whitebark Pine Seeds by Clark's Nutcracker: A Mutualism Hypothesis." *Journal of Animal Ecology* 51 (1982): 451–67.

Tomback, Diana F., and Peter Achuff. "Blister Rust and Western Forest Biodiversity: Ecology, Values, and Outlook for White Pines." *Forest Pathology* 40 (2010): 186–225.

Tomback, Diana F., Stephen F. Arno, and Robert E. Keane, eds. *Whitebark Pine Communities: Ecology and Restoration*. Washington, DC: Island Press, 2001.

Tomback, Diana F., and Katherine C. Kendall. "Biodiversity Losses: The Downward Spiral." In *Whitebark Pine Communities: Ecology and Restoration*, edited by Diana F. Tomback, Stephen F. Arno, and Robert E. Keane, 243–62. Washington, DC: Island Press, 2001.

Tronstad, Lusha M., Robert O. Hall Jr., Todd M. Koel, and Ken G. Gerow. "Introduced Lake Trout Produced a Four-Level Trophic Cascade in

Yellowstone Lake." *Transactions of the American Fisheries Society* 139 (2010): 1536–50.

U.S. Fish and Wildlife Service. "Endangered and Threatened Wildlife and Plants; 12-Month Finding on a Petition to List *Pinus albicaulis* as Endangered or Threatened with Critical Habitat." Department of the Interior, 42631–54. *Federal Register* 76, no. 138 (July 19, 2011).

U.S. Fish and Wildlife Service. "Endangered and Threatened Wildlife and Plants; 12-Month Finding on a Petition to List Rio Grande Cutthroat Trout as an Endangered or Threatened Species." Department of the Interior, 59140–50. *Federal Register* 79, no. 190 (October 1, 2014).

U.S. Fish and Wildlife Service. "Endangered and Threatened Wildlife and Plants; 12-Month Finding for a Petition to List the Yellowstone Cutthroat Trout as Threatened." Department of the Interior, 8818–31. *Federal Register* 71, no. 34 (February 21, 2006).

Varley, John D. "A History of Fish Stocking Activities in Yellowstone National Park between 1881 and 1980." Information Paper no. 35. Yellowstone National Park, WY, January 1, 1981.

Varley, John D., and Paul Schullery. *Yellowstone Fishes: Ecology, History, and Angling in the Park*. Mechanicsburg, PA: Stackpole Books, 1998.

Varley, John D., and Paul Schullery. "The Yellowstone Lake Crisis: Confronting a Lake Trout Invasion." Yellowstone National Park, WY: Yellowstone Center for Resources, 1995.

Varley, John D., and Paul Schullery. "Yellowstone Lake and Its Cutthroat Trout." In *Science and Ecosystem Management in the National Parks*, edited by William L. Halvorson and Gary E. Davis, 49–73. Tucson: University of Arizona Press, 1996.

Walker, Brian, and David Salt. *Resilience Thinking: Sustaining Ecosystems and People in a Changing World.* Washington, DC: Island Press, 2006.

Warwell, Marcus V., Gerald E. Rehfeldt, and Nicholas L. Crookston. "Modeling Contemporary Climate Profiles of Whitebark Pine (*Pinus albicaulis*) and Predicting Responses to Global Warming." USDA Forest Service Report, R6-NR-FHP-2007-01, 2007, 139–142.

Whittlesey, Lee H. "Of Fairies' Wings and Fish: Fishery Operations and the Lake Fish Hatchery in Yellowstone." *Yellowstone Science* 14, no. 2 (2006): 13–17.

Wiley, Robert W. *Wyoming Fish Management, 1869–1993, Administrative Report.* Cheyenne: Wyoming Game and Fish Department, 1993.

Wilkinson, Charles F. *Crossing the Next Meridian: Land, Water, and the Future of the West.* Washington, DC: Island Press, 1992.

Wolf, Evan C., David J. Cooper, and N. Thompson Hobbs. "Hydrologic Regime and Herbivory Stabilize an Alternative State in Yellowstone National Park." *Ecological Applications* 17, no. 6 (2007): 1572–87.

Wyoming Game and Fish Department. *Bighorn Herd Unit M313, Job Completion Report, Hunt Areas 1, 34, 42 43.* Cheyenne: Wyoming Game and Fish Department, 2009.

AUTHOR BIOGRAPHY

Bradley Johnson was raised in rural Wyoming, often making trips to his family's log cabin in the Bighorn Mountains, a place of profound solace and refuge for him.

Johnson graduated from the University of Wyoming in 2003 with a bachelor's degree in political science. He then served with the US Army in Iraq, after which he attended graduate school, earning a master's degree in political science and a PhD in natural resource and environmental studies from the University of New Hampshire.

Since 2010, Johnson has been working in the field of natural resource management in Colorado and his home state of Wyoming. He remains an avid fly fisherman.

Made in the USA
Lexington, KY
17 September 2017